Klaus Wolfsperger
Annette Miehle-Wolfsperger

Walks on Tenerife

Translated by Andrea Adelung and Tom Krupp

52 selected walks on the coasts and in the mountains
of the »Island of the Blissful«

With 89 colour photos,
52 Freytag & Berndt walking maps with a scale of 1:50,000 / 1:75,000 and
four overview maps with a scale of 1:250,000 / 1:500,000

ROTHER · MUNICH

Front cover:
The »Finger of God« (Roques de García) with Pico del Teide in the background.

Frontispiece (photo on page 2):
Descent to the Paisaje Lunar – one of the classic tours of the island.

All photos are by the authors.

Cartography:
Walking maps with a scale of 1:50,000 / 1:75,000 and
overview maps 1:250,000 / 1:500,000
© Freytag & Berndt, Vienna

Translation:
Andrea Adelung and Tom Krupp (revised and updated translation)

The descriptions of all the walks given in this guide are made according
to the best knowledge of the authors. The use of this guide is at one's
own risk. As far as is legally permitted, no responsibility will be accepted
for possible accidents, damage or injury of any kind.

2nd edition 2004
© Bergverlag Rother GmbH, Munich

ISBN 3-7633-4809-3

Distributed in Great Britain by Cordee, 3a De Montfort Street, Leicester
Great Britain LE1 7HD, www.cordee.co.uk

ROTHER WALKING GUIDES

Algarve · Andalusia South · Azores · Bernese Oberland East · Corsica · Côte d'Azur ·
Crete East · Crete West · Cyprus · Gomera · Gran Canaria · Iceland · La Palma · Madeira · Mallorca ·
Mont Blanc · Norway South · Provence · Pyrenees 1, 2, 3 · Sardinia · Sicily · High Tatra · Tenerife ·
Tuscany North · Valais East · Valais West · Vanoise · Around the Zugspitze

**Dear mountain lovers! We would be happy to hear your opinion
and suggestions for amendment to this Rother walking guide.**

BERGVERLAG ROTHER · Munich
D-85521 Ottobrunn · Haidgraben 3 · Tel. (089) 608669-0, Fax -69
Internet www.rother.de · **E-mail** bergverlag@rother.de

Preface

Tenerife can be described as the most diverse walking paradise of the Canary Islands – not only due to the Pico del Teide, at 3718 m, the highest peak in the Canary Island archipelago and in all of Spain, but also because of the numerous landscapes united on the island: the extremely barren, almost desert-like south is primarily frequented by beach-going tourists but the area around Adeje, Arona and the valley of San Lorenzo does boast a few beautiful walking destinations with dramatic *barrancos* and grand panoramic summits. In the fertile north, the countryside is dominated by agriculture: lush gardens, banana plantations, friendly villages and towns, plus a plunging coastline, characterise this picturesque region, contributing to one of Tenerife's epithets – »Island of Eternal Spring«. On the northern side of the Anaga and Teno Mountains, countless laurel and heath woods can be found, and the slopes of the Cumbre Dorsal, as well as the area around the caldera, are blanketed by vast pine forests. The climax of the experience is, without a doubt, the »lunar landscape« of the Cañadas del Teide National Park.

This guide offers walkers a wide variety of entertaining tour recommendations taking all the regions of the island into account. The selection, always offering panoramic views of the vast, deep-blue sea, ranges from pleasant paths to precipitous cliffs, from tranquil mountain rambles to panoramic summit climbs – walking paths through enchanting, primeval cloud forests are included, as are the sometimes stone-paved *caminos* which formed the main linking routes between the villages in days gone by. Several tour recommendations are also excellent choices for less experienced hikers. Veteran mountain hikers, who do not shy away from »extreme« walks and enjoy a shot of adventure and excitement, will also find a rich selection of tours: daring cliff hikes, spectacular gorge walks and lengthy mountain treks, whose highlights are definitely the centrepiece summits of the national parks. Despite the variety of tours, this guide leaves mountain enthusiasts enough space for their own discoveries.

A few new routes have been added to this edition which has been thoroughly updated at the same time – not least thanks to many friendly letters which we have received from our readers. Forest fires, road construction and the steady encroachments of Nature, however, cause constant changes – thus, we kindly ask you to write to the publishers concerning any corrections or additions that need to be made.

We wish you a pleasant and eventful holiday on the »Island of the Blissful«.

Summer 2004   Klaus and Annette Wolfsperger

Contents

Tourist Information

Use of this guide

The description of each route is preceded by a list of the most important information in abbreviated form. The course of each route is marked on the coloured hiking maps. All walking destinations, locations, starting and finishing points and all important points en route are listed in the index at the back of the book. Overview maps pinpoint the locations of the individual walks.

Grade

Most of the walks follow distinct trails and paths, however, this should not detract from the fact that some walks demand physical fitness, sure-footedness, a head for heights and a good sense of direction. Keep in mind that difficulties can be greatly increased by inclement weather. To better judge the difficulties of individual tours, the route recommendations (walk numbers) are colour-coded as follows:

BLUE These walks follow paths which are generally wide enough for easy walking, only moderately steep and thus relatively harmless, even in poor weather. They may also be undertaken by children and older walkers without great danger.

RED These walks follow trails and mountain paths that are generally narrow and even exposed over short stretches. Thus, such routes should only be undertaken by mountain hikers who are sure-footed. Short passages may even require greater demands on the walker's orientation skills.

BLACK These walks are frequently narrow and steep. In places, they can be extremely exposed and/or pose a danger of slipping when crossing over steep slopes, however, only in the rarest of cases will scrambling actually be involved. This means that such routes should only be undertaken by physically fit mountain hikers who have alpine hiking experience and a good sense of direction.

Dangers

Most routes follow well-maintained, distinct paths. In cases of extreme exposure or difficult walking, the text makes reference to such hazards. Thick fog, caused by the trade winds, can be expected on mountain slopes and ridges, especially from midday on. The clouds usually do not disperse again until the evening and can pose considerable orientation problems for mountain walkers. In addition, extremely strong and gusty winds often develop on the mountain ridges comparable to the *föhn* winds of the Alps. After strong rains, it is wise to avoid *barrancos* and slippery mountain slopes.

Pico del Teide

In every sense, the highpoint of Tenerife (Walk 51 – can be combined with Pico Viejo, Walk 52; 6¼ alternatively 8¼ hrs).

Guajara

The most beautiful panoramic summit on the rim of the caldera (Walk 47; 4½ hrs).

Masca Gorge

A »must«: the most famous gorge of the Canary Islands (Walk 23; 5½ hrs).

Paisaje Lunar

The »lunar landscape« – one of the most fascinating natural wonders of the island (Walk 48; 1¾ hrs).

Great Faro de Anaga Circuit

Wonderful circuit tour on the north-eastern tip (Walk 39; 4¾ hrs).

Candelaria Trail

Traversing the Cumbre Dorsal from the west to the east (Walks 8 and 9; 5 hrs).

From Arona to Adeje

A mountain trail full of variety along the south-western coast (Walk 26; 5¾ hrs).

From Buenavista to Masca

Via the spectacular Risco Trail to Teno Alto and then over the Tabaiba Pass to Masca (Walks 20, 19 and 18; 5 hrs).

From Chamorga to El Bailadero

Ridgeline hike through the primeval cloud forest (Walk 37, if desired, in combination with Walk 36; 2¾ or 4¼ hrs).

From Punta del Hidalgo to Batán

Adventurous circuit walk for hikers with strong nerves (Walk 30; 4½ hrs).

Órganos Trail

Spectacular circuit route in the upper Orotava Valley (Walk 5; 4 hrs).

From Las Carboneras to Taganana

Impressive route passing over the Playa de Tamadite (Walks 33 and 34; 5 hrs).

Best time of year

Tenerife is a year-round travel destination, however in the winter months the weather is not quite as stable as in the summer. During this time, snowfall in elevations of 1500 m and heavy rain showers are not uncommon.

Equipment

Sturdy shoes with non-slip soles, durable trousers, sunscreen and possibly a sun hat, protective gear for wind, rain and cold, as well as hiking provisions (sufficient liquids) are required for most tours.

Walking times

The times indicated represent only the actual walking time – not including breaks for a rest or photos! Usually the times for the individual stages and total walking times will be cited.

Food and accommodation

With the exception of the Refugio de Altavista (staffed in the summer months, self-service; winter room available), there are no huts. A speciality are the *chozas* – covered picnic places furnished with tables and benches.

Approach

Most of the walks are accessible with public transport but sometimes a private vehicle must be used. A timetable for the main bus lines can be found on page 16, however, it is best to acquire timetables at the local bus depots or at tourist offices.

Emergency phone number

The general emergency number for the police, the fire brigade and urgent medical attention is © 112.

Maps

The walking maps with the routes highlighted on them and with a scale of 1:50,000 / 1:75,000) that preface each tour recommendation are an essential feature of this guide. For those who want to obtain other maps, we recommend the road and walking map from Freytag & Berndt with a scale of 1:75,000, or the Kompass hiking map on a scale of 1:50,000. More detailed, but sometimes less up to date are the 8-part military map series with a scale of 1:50,000 and the 21-part military map series with a scale of 1:25,000, locally available at the Equipo de Geodesia y Cartográfia, Calle Rambla de Puido 1, Santa Cruz de Tenerife (Mon – Fri 8 a.m. – 2 p.m.; bring identification!). The Instituto Geográfico Nacional offers 20 more recent maps with a scale of 1:25,000, unfortunately drawn with only a few trails included – available locally at the Centro Geofisico, Calle La Marina 20 II, Santa Cruz de Tenerife (Mon – Fri 8 a.m. – 2 p.m.).

Environmental conservation

Please respect all plants and animals, never leave litter behind (what you take with you, take away with you!), do not carelessly throw away cigarette stubs and do not make open fires – forest fires are not uncommon on Tenerife.

Tips for linear and long-distance walkers

Some routes suggested are conceived as linear walks with destinations far away from the starting points. For these, we recommend to either use public transportation (bus, taxi), join an organised walking tour or make arrangements with a walker with another car. In this case, the best arrangement is to drop one car off at the destination then car-pool to the starting point; another method is to meet the other walker/driver en route, switch car keys and then pick up the other car at the end to drive to some prearranged point to swap back again (a well thought-out plan is essential here!).

On Tenerife, long-distance hikers will find good possibilities for treks with one or more overnight sojourns, especially in the Anaga and Teno Mountains but also in the Cañadas (crossing Teide!) and in the forest/volcano belt north-west of Teide. Generally, however, overnight accommodation is almost non-existent, so we recommend taking along at least a sleeping bag and a bivouac shelter. Shopping possibilities en route are also often limited.

Walking on Tenerife

The most diverse of the Canary Islands

As are all the other islands in the Canary archipelago, Tenerife is of volcanic origin. In terms of its area (2057 km^2) as well as its elevation (3718 m), Tenerife by far surpasses all of the other islands – the landscape is accordingly diverse, ranging from the desert-like south to the damp north with its lush forests in middle elevations and to the sub-alpine mountain region around Pico del Teide.

The heart of the island is Pico del Teide and its dramatic caldera, with a diameter of about 16 km. It also presents the youngest part of the island which, millions of years ago, started out as two islands, now the Anaga and the Teno mountain ranges, that were subsequently joined through the upsurge of the Cumbre Dorsal and the caldera.

Flora and fauna

Tenerife consists of several completely different zones of vegetation depending on the altitude as well as climatic conditions. The flora is accordingly diverse and includes countless endemics (plants found exclusively on the island). In the coastal regions, several modest desert plants thrive: dragon trees

The pride of the Tinerfeños: red and blue »tower of jewels«.

11

Shelter (choza) in the Orotava Valley.

and palm trees are common here, however, succulents predominate the landscape (spurge and cacti). Bananas are one of the most important economic products of the island; plantations of these cultivated plants, intensively irrigated and subsidised by the State as well as the EU, cover vast parts of the coastal regions up to an elevation of about 300 m. About 20 % of the island is covered by forest: the dense, jungle-like laurel forest (laurisilva forest), with the exception of a few remnants in the Anaga and Teno mountains, has been almost completely destroyed – most of the rest grows on the damp northern and eastern slopes and gorges. Above the laurel forest is the fayal-brezal zone (tree heaths and gale) and the sparse pine forests on the western and southern slopes. The Canary pine (Pinus canariensis) is extremely fire resistant and can survive even the most severe forest fire. In elevations above 2000 m, the broom-like laburnum bushes, bearing yellow blossoms in early summer, and the white-blossoming Teide broom dominate the landscape. Another speciality of the Cañadas is the lavishly-blooming, up to 2-m high Teide »tower of jewels«, found at elevations up to 2800 m and the Teide violet which can be found at elevations up to 3000 m.

The only mammals encountered in the mountains with any regularity are rabbits and rodents. Moufflon (Barbary sheep) are also very common in the Teide National Park, although they are rarely seen.

National Park (Parque Nacional de las Cañadas del Teide)

The Parque Nacional de las Cañadas del Teide was established in 1954. It primarily includes the entire crater area and, with 20,000 ha and a circumference of approximately 75 km, is one of the largest national parks in Spain and one of the most visited. It is divided into several zones of conservation. In general, all plants and animals, and also the bizarre stone formations, are protected. In addition, wandering from the official walking paths and camping in the wild are prohibited. A brochure from the state-run National Park Commission provides detailed information on conservation regulations. There are small exhibits at the visitor centres at El Portillo and Parador (Cañada Blanca) on the history and geology of the caldera and Teide; visitors may, on request, participate in guided walks.

Animal Parks

The Loro Parque in Puerto de la Cruz houses the largest collection of parrots in the world (about 300 types) – dolphins, sea lions, crocodiles, penguins, apes and sharks are also on display here. There is a butterfly park in Icod de Los Vinos.

Botanical Gardens

The Jardín Botánico in Puerto de la Cruz presents luxuriant tropical and subtropical flora. In the Bananera El Guanche near Puerto de la Cruz, banana farming is explored in detail. The Jardines del Atlántico near Buzanada (Valle de San Lorenzo) offer a sampling of the plant world on the Canary Islands. The Cactus Park near Los Cristianos boasts a large cactus collection.

Canyoning

The deeply-cut, mostly dry *barrancos* draw the visitor to adventurous gorge tours, e.g. Barranco del Infierno, del Río and the gorges of the Gigantes coastline cliffs (Barranco de Masca, del Carrizal, etc.) and in the Anaga Mountains.

Casinos

In Puerto de la Cruz and in Playa de las Américas.

Climbing

There are several worthwhile spots for climbing on the island: the Catedral and the Piedras Amarillas in the Cañadas, Arico (3 km in the direction of the Contador Valley), Las Vegas (near Granadilla), Guía de Isora (2.5 km in the direction of Adeje, then left towards Acojeja), Tabares (near Santa Cruz) as well as Mesa de Tejina.

Donkey and Dromedary Safaris

Donkey safaris (in Arafo, Buzanada and Santiago del Teide) and dromedary safaris (in El Tanque and Las Galletas) are popular excursions.

Golf

There are several golf courses, e.g. near Las Galletas and near Tacoronte.

Jeep Safaris

Jeep safaris mostly follow the dirt roads to the north-west of Teide.

Caves

Numerous caves exist – the most famous, Cueva del Viento near Icod, is reportedly open to the public.

Mountain Biking

This sport is becoming more and more popular. The island offers ideal conditions for easy as well as more strenuous tours especially around Teide National Park.

Museums

The Museo Arqueólogico in Santa Cruz houses, among other objects, a valuable collection of artefacts from the Guanche civilisation.

Pyramids of Güimar

The ethnographic park 'Pirámides de Güimar' displays step pyramids.

Sailing Tours

The »Nostramo« sails from Playa de San Juan to the coastline of Acantilado de los Gigantes.

Teide Cable Car

The cable car (2356 – 3555 m) is one of the Cañadas main attractions; no service during storms, snow or icy conditions.

Water Parks

The Lago Martiánez in Puerto de la Cruz, designed by César Manrique. In Las Américas, the Aguapark Octopus.

Information and Addresses

Getting there
Flights are available to Tenerife from all the major airports in Great Britain and Europe. There are ferry and flight connections to the Spanish mainland and to all of the other Canary Islands.

Information
Tourist information: Oficina de Turismo de Tenerife, Plaza de España, E-38003 Santa Cruz de Tenerife, ✆ 922 / 60 58 00.

Camping
There are only a few camping grounds (at Adeje, Las Galletas, Garachico, Puertito de Güímar and Punta del Hidalgo). Camping in the wild is not permitted.

Theft
The crime rate is relatively high, therefore never leave valuables unattended in a car or anywhere else.

Internet
The Rother homepage at www.rother.de (WebLinks) offers numerous useful links to internet information for the Canary Islands and Tenerife.

CLIMATE TABLE FOR PUERTO DE LA CRUZ													
Month		1	2	3	4	5	6	7	8	9	10	11	12	Year
Day	°C	19	19	20	21	22	23	24	26	26	24	22	20	22
Night	°C	13	13	14	14	16	18	19	20	20	18	17	14	16
Water	°C	19	19	19	19	20	20	22	23	22	22	21	20	20
Sunshine	hrs	5	6	7	8	9	10	11	10	8	6	6	5	7
Rainy days		10	7	8	4	3	2	1	1	3	5	7	9	5

Climber on the Piedras Amarillas in the Cañadas.

Climate
Tenerife is characterised by a subtropical climate with slight temperature fluctuations. The weather is determined by the trade winds which bring warm, moist air masses from the north-east that collect in the mountains and often cover large areas of the island, especially in the north, in a thick blanket of clouds.

Taxi
A taxi stand is located in almost all of the larger towns – otherwise, you can usually call for a taxi in a local bar.

Telephone
The dialling code for Spain / Tenerife is 0034 / 922. The dialling code for Great Britain from the Canary Islands is 0044, for the USA 001.

Organised Walks and Walking Guides
There are several walk organisers (ask in the hotels).

102   PUERTO DE LA CRUZ   –   SANTA CRUZ   (EXPRESS)

daily   5.45, 6.15, 6.30, 7.15–21.15 every 30 min, 23.00   6.00–20.30 every 30 min, 21.15, 22.30, 00.15

---

101   PUERTO DE LA CRUZ   –   SANTA CRUZ
(via La Orotava–Santa Ursula–La Victoria–La Matanza–Tacoronte–La Laguna)

Mon–Fri	5.30–21.00 every 30 min	6.00–21.30 every 30 min
Sat	5.30–13.30 every 30 min, 14.30–20.30 every hr	6.00–13.30 every 30 min, 14.30–21.30 every hr
Sun	5.30–13.30 every hr, 14.00–21.00 every 30 min	6.30–13.30 every hr, 14.00–21.30 every 30 min

---

343   PUERTO DE LA CRUZ   –   LAS AMERICAS   (EXPRESS)

daily   9.00, 11.10, 15.20, 17.35   9.00, 11.30, 15.30, 17.45

---

354   PUERTO DE LA CRUZ   –   ICOD DE LOS VINOS
(via Las Dehesas–Los Realejos–Icod Alto–La Guancha)

daily   6.20, 7.30–20.30 every hr, 21.45   5.15, 6.00–19.00 every hr, 20.10

---

325   PUERTO DE LA CRUZ   –   LOS GIGANTES   (via Icod d.l. Vinos)

daily   6.20, 10.40, 14.40, 19.15   8.40, 12.55, 17.15, 21.25

---

363   PUERTO DE LA CRUZ   –   BUENAVISTA
(via Las Arenas–Realejo Bajo–San Juan de la Rambla–Icod–Garachico–Los Silos)

daily   6.00–21.00 every hr   5.20, 6.30–20.30 every hr

---

345   PUERTO DE LA CRUZ   –   LA CALDERA
(via El Botánico–La Orotava–Aguamansa, only to/from ■ Orotava, ● Aguamansa)

daily   ■5.30, ■6.30, ●7.00, ●8.00, 8.45, 9.35, 10.20, 11.15, 11.45, 12.30, 13.15, 14.00, 15.00, 15.45, 16.30, 17.15, ●18.00, ●18.45, ●19.35, ●20.15, ■21.00, ■22.30   ●6.00, ●7.00, ●7.30, ●8.15, ●9.00, 9.45, 10.45, 11.30, 12.15, 12.50, 13.45, 14.20, 15.10, 16.10, 16.50, 17.40, 18.15, ●19.15, ●20.00, ■20.45, ●21.15

---

348   PUERTO DE LA CRUZ   –   LAS CAÑADAS (Parador Nacional)
(via El Botánico–La Orotava–Aguamansa–El Portillo–Teleférico)

daily   9.15   16.00

---

360   ICOD DE LOS VINOS   –   PUERTO DE ERJOS
(via El Amparo–La Vega–La Montañeta–San José de Los Llanos)

daily   7.15, 9.25, 11.30, 15.00, 18.30   7.50, 10.10, 12.15, 15.45, 19.10

---

460   ICOD DE LOS VINOS   –   LAS AMERICAS
(via El Tanque–Erjos–Santiago del Teide–Tamaimo–Chío–Guía de Isora)

daily   5.45, 7.30, 10.00, 12.00, 14.15, 16.00, 18.00, 20.10   5.25, 7.20, 9.45, 12.00, 13.55, 16.00, 18.00, 20.00

---

355   BUENAVISTA   –   SANTIAGO DEL TEIDE
(via El Palmar–Las Portelas–Masca; ● only to/from Masca)

Mon–Fri   ●6.15, 9.30, ●14.15, 15.45   ●6.45, 10.35, ●15.00, 16.55

---

366   BUENAVISTA   –   LAS PORTELAS   (via El Palmar)

Mon–Fri	5.30, 7.30, 9.30, 13.15, 17.30, 19.30	6.00, 8.00, 10.00, 14.00, 18.00, 20.00
Sat, Sun	5.30, 7.30, 11.30, 13.30, 15.15, 19.30	6.00, 8.00, 12.00, 14.00, 16.00, 20.00

473	**LAS GALLETAS (Costa Silencio)**	– **LOS GIGANTES**
	(via Los Cristianos–Las Américas–Adeje–Armeñime–San Juan–Alcalá–Puerto Santiago)	
daily	6.15, 6.45, 7.15, 7.45, 8.10–19.30 every 20 min, 19.45, 20.00, 20.45, 21.45	6.15, 6.45, 7.45, 8.15, 8.45, 9.15, 9.45, 10.15, 10.35, 11.05–20.05 every 20 min, 21.50, 22.30

482	**LOS CRISTIANOS**	– **VILAFLOR** (via Arona, La Escalona)
daily	6.00, 11.00, 17.00	6.35, 12.00, 18.15

342	**LAS AMERICAS**	– **LAS CAÑADAS** (El Portillo)
	(via Los Cristianos–Arona–La Escalona–Vilaflor–Parador Nacional–Teleférico)	
daily	9.15 (9.00 Torviscas, 9.30 Los Cristianos)	15.15 (15.40 Teleférico, 16.00 Parador)

111	**LAS AMERICAS**	– **SANTA CRUZ**
	(municipal bus via Los Cristianos–Autopista Sur)	
daily	6.00–22.00 every 30 min, 23.15, 00.30, 04.30	5.30–21.30 every 30 min, 22.30, 23.30, 02.30

121	**SANTA CRUZ**	– **GÜIMAR** (via Autopista Sur–Arafo)
Mon–Fri	6.15–20.15 every hr	5.45–20.45 every hr
Sat, Sun	7.45–19.45 every 2 hrs	5.45–19.45 every 2 hrs

105	**SANTA CRUZ**	– **PUNTA DEL HIDALGO**
	(via Autopista Norte–La Laguna–Las Canteras–Tegueste–Tejina–Bajamar)	
daily	5.15, 5.45, 6.15, 6.40, 7.35–19.35 every 30 min, 20.15, 20.55 (La Laguna approx. 10 min later)	6.05, 6.40, 7.15, 7.40, 8.00–20.00 every 30 min, 21.00, 21.30, 22.00

246	**SANTA CRUZ**	– **TAGANANA** (– Almáciga)
	(via San Andrés–Cruce El Bailedero)	(leaves Almáciga approx. 10 min earlier)
Mon–Fri	4.55, 6.50, 10.30, 13.10, 14.15, 17.05, 19.15	5.55, 8.00, 11.50, 14.30, 15.40, 18.20, 20.35
Sat, Sun	7.05, 9.10, 11.40, 14.15, 17.05, 20.15	8.15, 10.40, 12.55, 15.40, 18.20, 21.30

247	**SANTA CRUZ**	– **CHAMORGA** (via El Bailedero)
Mon–Fri	5.00, 15.00, 18.00 (Sa 7.30, 15.00, 18.00)	6.15, 16.30, 19.30 (Sa 8.50, 16.30, 19.30)

245	**SANTA CRUZ**	– **IGUESTE** (via San Andrés–Teresitas)
Mon–Fri	5.20, 7.25, 9.15, 11.50, 14.10, 16.10, 18.15, 20.30	6.45, 8.05, 10.10, 12.30, 15.10–21.10 every 2 hrs
Sat, Sun	6.40, 8.40, 10.40, 12.30–20.30 every 2 hrs	7.30–21.30 every 2 hrs

073	**LA LAGUNA**	– **PICO DEL INGLES** (via Cruz del Carmen)
Mon–Fri	10.45, 14.45 (Sat, Sun 9.15, 11.00)	11.10, 15.10 (Sat, Sun 9.40, 11.25)

074	**LA LAGUNA**	– **EL BATAN** (via Cruce El Moquinal)
Mon–Fri	7.00, 9.05 (Sat, Sun), 14.10 (Sat, Sun), 14.45, 19.05	7.45, 9.50 (Sat, Sun), 15.00 (Sat, Sun), 15.45, 19.50

075	**LA LAGUNA**	– **TABORNO** (Las Carboneras 15 min earlier)
Mon–Fri	5.00, 6.45, 9.15, 13.05, 15.15, 18.45	5.45, 7.45, 10.00, 14.00, 16.15, 19.45
Sat, Sun	7.30, 12.15, 16.05	8.10, 13.15, 17.00

076	**LA LAGUNA**	– **AFUR** (via Las Canteras–C.d. Carmen)
daily	6.55, 13.15, 16.05, 19.00 (Mon–Fri)	5.45, 7.55, 14.45, 17.30, 20.00 (Mon–Fri)

077	**LA LAGUNA**	– **EL BAILADERO** (via Cruz del Carmen)
daily	10.15, 17.00 (Mon–Fri), 18.00 (Sat, Sun)	11.30, 18.00 (Mon–Fri), 19.15 (Sat, Sun)

TITSA timetable available at the local bus depots or at tourist offices, Internet: www.titsa.com

The Northern Island

Garden landscape at the foot of the Cumbre

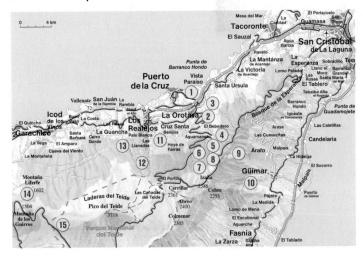

The northern island is the garden of Tenerife: banana plantations along the coasts and near the quaint villages characterise this traditional farming region on both sides of the Cumbre Dorsal and on the northern foot of Teide.

Visitors travelling on the motorway from La Laguna heading to the northern side of the Cumbre and down to the almost 10-km wide Orotava Valley will immediately be impressed by the sprawling countryside gently sloping to the sea and towered over by Teide – sometimes snow-covered in winter. Puerto de la Cruz is the tourist centre of the region. This fashionable and perhaps the most beautiful seaside resort of the island offers the holidaymaker ideal conditions for an entertaining sojourn: a diverse selection of tourist activities, beautiful gardens, majestic cliffs with picturesque beaches and excellent public transportation connections. Many walkers favour Puerto due to its proximity to the forests of the upper Orotava Valley – those preferring more diverse walking routes choose the higher elevations of the Cumbre Dorsal and the foot of Teide, following beautiful walking trails starting from the Orotava Valley. The southern side of Cumbre Dorsal, especially the Güímar Valley, surrounded by two mighty cliffs, is also connected via a few worthwhile walking routes. West of the Orotava Valley, extensive pine forests can be found in the higher elevations, breaking abruptly at the sand and lava terrain found at the

The Orotava Valley undergoes intensive agriculture.

foot of Teide and Pico Viejo – an almost limitless, still widely undiscovered walking region!

The beaches also prove to be a dream come true – especially Camello Beach near Mesa del Mar, Jardín Beach and Bollullo Bay near Puerto de la Cruz, Socorro Beach near La Rambla and San Marcos Beach near Icod de los Vinos. Be forewarned of the one thing that all beaches have in common – an exceptionally dangerous surf, especially in winter.

STARTING POINTS FOR WALKS

La Orotava–El Portillo Road

This road which leads through the rural Orotava Valley and through the pine forest belt from Aguamansa on to El Portillo – the north-eastern entrance to the Parque Nacional de las Cañadas del Teide – is an ideal starting point for walks in the upper Orotava Valley. Some of the car parks for walkers located along the way are Aguamansa (trout hatchery and forester's house, km 15), turn-off to the La Caldera picnic area (barbecue and picnic sites, km 16), Choza Bermeja (km 21), Choza Wildpret (km 23.5), Choza Bethencourt (km 25.9) and Choza Sventenius (km 29.2).

Cumbre Dorsal Ridge Road

The ridge road connecting La Laguna with La Esperanza, Izaña and El Portillo not only boasts numerous *miradores*, offering wonderful downward views of the northern and eastern coasts, but also starting points for lovely walking excursions through the Esperanza Forest (e.g. from the Las Lagunetas picnic area to Gaitero, 1¾ hrs) and into the Güímar and upper Orotava Valleys.

Other ideal starting points are the picnic areas Chanajiga (Las Llanadas), La Corona (Icod el Alto), El Lagar (La Guancha), Las Arenas Negras (La Montañeta).

1 From Puerto de la Cruz to the Café Vista Paraíso

Walk on the Camino de la Costa along the coastline cliffs

Puerto de la Cruz – La Paz – Playa del Bollullo – El Rincón – Café Vista Paraíso and back

Starting point: Puerto de la Cruz, 15 m, Playa de Martiánez on the east end of Puerto's seaside promenade (point of departure for free bus service and the open-air shuttle »train« to Loro Parque).

Walking times: Puerto de la Cruz – Mirador de la Paz 20 min, Mirador de la Paz – Playa del Bollullo 1 hr, Playa del Bollullo – Café Vista Paraíso 1 hr, return route 1¾ hrs; total time a good 4 hrs.

Ascent: About 350 m.

Grade: Easy walk on wide trails and roads – only the ascent to Café Vista Paraíso is made on a steep, narrow path.

Refreshment: Restaurant and café/bar »Bollullo« at Bollullo Bay, café/restaurant »San Diego«, café »Vista Paraíso«, bars and restaurants in Cuesta de la Villa.

The well-maintained, mostly paved Camino de la Costa is one of the most popular walking trails in Puerto – leading from Mirador de la Paz along a charming panoramic promenade to the hotel »Semiramis« and from there through banana plantations to what is probably the north's most beautiful beach, Playa del Bollullo. Due to the dangerous undercurrents and a powerful surf, the fine-sand beach is only suitable for swimming during calm seas. From here, we recommend ascending to one of the most famous panoramic spots in Tenerife, the café »Vista Paraíso«.

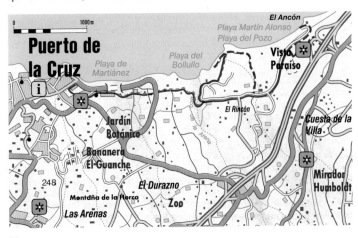

Majestic start: the Camino de la Costa runs high along the cliffs of Puerto de la Cruz. In the background, the sea water swimming pools.

From **Martiánez Beach**, walk up, passing between the hotels San Felipe and Atlantis along the palm-lined avenue *Avenida Aguilar y Quesada* and, past the Martiánez shopping center (on your left, 5 min), reach the palm-planted square *Plaza Viera y Clavijo* then turn left onto the stepped trail *Camino las Cabras* – this connects the old town with the districts of La Paz and El Botánico. A few minutes later, merge into a wider promenade (*Camino San Amaro*) and continue the ascent to the left. Benches on the stepped trail repeatedly offer the walker nice spots for a break. 5 minutes later, reach a road and turn left toward **Mirador de la Paz**.

Enjoying a tremendous downward view of Puerto de la Cruz and the Martiánez Beach, now continue above the cliffs along the balcony-like *Camino de la Costa*, passing several cafés and apartment houses. At the hotel »Semiramis« (a total of ½ hr) the *camino* merges into the *Calle Leopoldo Cólogan Zulueta*; here turn left. Via the *Camino La Costa* continue straight on. Soon leave the last villas and holiday apartments behind (bear left at a fork). At first the wide pedestrian walkway continues along above the eastbound arterial road leading out of town but soon passes under it to the left through a tunnel. Now we are surrounded by banana plantations. About 10 min after the tunnel, cross the Barranco de la Arena to reach a lane on the other side of the *barranco* and continue straight on along this (to the right on the edge of the *barranco* – the path leading to the café »Vista Paraíso«). After just a few minutes, at the restaurant »Bollullo«, a path branches off to the left, leading high above **Playa del Bollullo** along the cliffs – on the east end of the beautiful, sandy bay, a broad stairway leads down to the beach where a snack bar is located. Incidentally, above the cliffs, an overgrown path leads further along and, after a good 5 min, turns to the right towards a small *barranco* then leads through it and finally ascends to the street in El Rincón (a possible short-cut to the café »Vista Paraíso«).

Back at the edge of Barranco de la Arena, walk uphill along the lane, bearing left. After not quite 15 min, pass the café/restaurant »San Diego« (closed Mondays) in the hamlet of **El Rincón**. To the right, on the wide asphalt street, you can ascend to La Orotava, however, continue straight on between the banana and avocado plantations. After 15 min, the road is blocked off by a chain (possible descent to the beautiful although tiny strip of beach Playa del Ancón:

Bollulo Beach is one of the most beautiful sand bays on the island, however, during the winter months, expect to confront a strong surf.

View down from the ascent route to café »Vista Paraíso« – below, we see the scattered hamlet of El Rincón, in the foreground to the right, Ancón Bay, and beyond it, Bollullo Bay; in the background, the »skyline« of Puerto de la Cruz.

starting along a track, after a few minutes bear left on a descending *camino* which ends as a footpath and steep steps, ¼ hr). Directly past the chain, the ascent route to the café »Vista Paraíso« branches off to the right, leading between walls. Ascend steeply for a few minutes and, at the first opportunity, take a short turn to the right to join up with the former main trail. Sometimes stone-paved, this continues a zigzag ascent steeply to the left. After a short stretch of steps, the path merges into a road in a villa settlement that brings us to the left to the traditional, German/Austrian café **Vista Paraíso** (150 m; closed Mondays). Delicious cakes and a magnificent view of Puerto de la Cruz and the Orotava Valley from the terrace make up for the strenuous ascent. If you do not wish to return to Puerto via the same route, you may continue the ascent on the wide trail diagonally across from the café. This soon merges with a road that leads along the northbound motorway. Head on the road to the left, then to the right over the bridge (motorway exit La Orotava) to Cuesta de la Villa. On the main road there is a bus stop directly to the right (line 062 to La Orotava and line 101 to Puerto de la Cruz; 10 min from the café Vista Paraíso).

2 From Aguamansa to La Orotava

Descent through the rural Orotava Valley to Las Cuevas

Aguamansa – Pinoleris – La Florida – Las Cuevas (La Orotava)

Farmers at rest.

Location: Aguamansa, 1000 m.
Starting point: Trout hatchery on the hairpin bend above Aguamansa, 1070 m (car park for walkers; bus stop for line 345).
Destination: Las Cuevas, 300 m, near La Orotava (bus stop for line 101).
Walking times: Aguamansa – La Florida 1½ hrs, La Florida – Las Cuevas ½ hr; total time 2 hrs.
Descent: 800 m.
Grade: Easy, sometimes steep descent, mostly on asphalt roads.
Refreshment: Bar/restaurants in Aguamansa, bar in La Florida and, at the final destination – bar/restaurant »Las Cuevas«.

Alternative: From Las Cuevas to Puerto de la Cruz: To the left next to the former café »Humboldtblick« (house no. 25), descend on a steep street for a good 5 min to the lower main road between La Orotava and Santa Ursula. Turn left onto this road and continue downhill, 5 min later, to the right through a tunnel under the motorway and then to the right on a wide road (pedestrian walkway) down to El Rincón. Merging with an intersecting street (café/restaurant »San Diego«; a good ½ hr from Las Cuevas) continue to the left to Puerto de la Cruz following Walk 1 (a good 1¼ hrs to Martiánez Beach).
Combination possible with Walk 4.

This mostly pleasant walk leads along country lanes that are sometimes somewhat steep, past potato fields and vineyards down to La Orotava.
The trail begins between the pools of the **trout hatchery** and leaves the premises through a gate in the wall a short distance on. After 30 m go to the right, through the gate and 150 m further on, through another gate down to the main

road. Follow this road 50 m to the left to the bus stop where the steep village street of Aguamansa branches off to the right. After just a few minutes, a slightly ascending lane branches off this street sharply to the right. This passes through a small *barranco* and a second one shortly afterwards. After a total of ½ hr, reach an intersection and take a left to continue the descent. A few minutes later at a shrine, a lane branches off to the right leading down to Choza Perez Ventoso (sign, →Walk 3), however, continue straight ahead. After a good 100 m, the lane branches again, this time to the left. After about 5 min, turn right onto Los Cominos lane which leads along on the level and then turns down to the left. The lane now leads steeply downwards in bends to a wider road (with a bar to the right); follow this to the left, past a picnic area, to the church of **Pinoleris**, 750 m.

Past the church, a steep road branches off to the right (sign »La Florida«) which swings to the right a good 5 min later and soon after leads past the bar »Florida Alta«. Continue downhill on this steep village street – after 10 min, it merges with a small street near a chapel; continue along this to reach **La Florida**.

Walking past the church and a schoolhouse with a playing field, reach a crossroad at a kiosk (to the left, the bus stop for La Orotava); turn to the right here. The road crosses a *barranco* and after 10 min passes a large, round water reservoir on the left. Just after, at the lowest point of the road, turn left onto the lane *La Resbala* which leads downhill. Bear right at the turn-off 5 min later, passing a rectangular reservoir. Just after passing it, take a left at the fork in the road and cross under an aqueduct. Now head straight on downhill (do not take the villa road branching off to the left) until reaching an intersection past a high tension pylon; here turn left onto the main road from La Orotava to Santa Ursula, passing the former café »Humboldtblick« (house no. 25 on the other side of the street) in **Las Cuevas**.

3   From Aguamansa to La Orotava via Pino Alto

Strenuous day walk over the eastern cliff face of the Orotava Valley

Aguamansa – Barranco del Infierno – Choza Almadi – Cruz de las Lajitas – Pino Alto – Las Cuevas (La Orotava)

Starting point: Trout hatchery, 1070 m, on the hairpin bend above Aguamansa (car park for walkers; bus stop for line 345).

Destination: Las Cuevas, 300 m, near La Orotava (bus stop for line 101).

Walking times: Aguamansa – Llano de los Corrales 1¼ hrs, Llano de los Corrales – Choza Almadi a good 1¼ hrs, Choza Almadi – Pino Alto a good 2 hrs, Pino Alto – Las Cuevas ½ hr; total time 5 hrs.

Ascent: 450 m and 1250 m in descent.

Grade: Strenuous day walk along trails and forestry roads; from Choza Almadi on, sometimes steep and unpleasantly slippery. The *ladera* is frequently shrouded by clouds brought in by the trade winds.

Refreshment: Bar/restaurants at the La Caldera picnic area, in Pino Alto and in Las Cuevas.

Alternative: Begin the walk at the picnic area La Caldera: follow →Walk 4 to Choza El Topo (not quite 1 hr) and then straight on along the forestry road to the stone column Llano de los Corrales (a good 10 min).

Admittedly, this hike along a forestry road above the eastern, often cloud-covered cliff face of the Orotava Valley is somewhat of a plod and also quite strenuous. Only from time to time some very fine views of the Orotava Valley open up, otherwise we are surrounded by lofty lichen-covered pines.

Initially, the route is identical with →Walk 2 (please refer). After a good half hour, by the shrine, turn left onto the lane (sign »Choza Perez Ventoso«) that ends 5 min later at the stone column *Choza Perez Ventoso*. Here, ascend to the left on the steep forestry trail and then after reaching the trail junction below **Choza Inge Jua** (5 min; to the right a possible ascent to Choza El Topo, ¼ hr) take the forestry trail leading straight, almost on the level, into the Barranco del Infierno. After 5 min, the track narrows to a footpath at a small turnabout (straight ahead) and soon crosses a stream bed then on the other side of the valley ascends steeply in zigzags. A good 10 min later, the *camino* broadens into a wider forestry track. Some minutes later, at the stone column Llano de los Corrales, meet up with a wide forestry road.

Turn left onto the forestry road. The road ascends in eight broad bends along the edge of the Barranco del Infierno (these can be circumvented via a distinct path) and after an hour leads in easy up-and-down walking along the steep cliff wall of the *ladera*. Here is a good opportunity to find a spot to take a break and enjoy a superb view of the Cumbre Dorsal, Teide and across the Orotava Valley to the coast – later on, at **Choza Almadi**, 1470 m (shelter, stone column) pine trees block the views.

At the shelter, turn left on a forestry road. This descends steeply along the *ladera* and, after 20 min, reaches the most spectacular overlook of the entire route – the **Cruz de las Lajitas** (cross, shrine, shelter). From the platform, relish a boundless bird's-eye view of the Orotava Valley. At the other end of the *mirador*, the steep road continues the descent. The route now always leads along the sheer edge of the *ladera*; subsequently, always continue straight ahead respectively left at forks, as well as at the fork reached in a quarter hour (to the left continuing on the level) and in the right bend that follows (turn left onto the forestry track). 5 min later bear again to the left. At the next right bend that follows, take the left fork onto a footpath. This descends in zigzag bends (sometimes overgrown and slippery) and after a good 10 min, just before reaching a wrecked car, merges into a track (turn right; the track is sometimes cemented) that gently descends straight on through terraces with countless chestnut trees. After 25 min, the track reaches a barrier and a shrine and then merges into a road. Follow this to the left to enjoy a stunning view of the Orotava Valley and Puerto de la Cruz; after 20 min of descent reach the village street of **Pino Alto**, 580 m.

Here, turn left and descend steeply, soon leaving the picturesque hamlet behind. After a good 10 min, at the lowest point of the road, turn right onto the lane *La Resbala* which is flanked by walls (straight ahead along the road, after a good 5 min, to the right over a bridge – La Florida; bus stop). Bear right at the turn-off 5 min later, passing a rectangular reservoir. Just after passing it, take a left at the fork in the road and cross under an aqueduct. Now head straight on downhill (do not take the villa road branching off to the left) until reaching an intersection past a high tension pylon; here turn left onto the main road from La Orotava to Santa Ursula, passing the former café »Humboldtblick« (house no. 25 on the other side of the street) in **Las Cuevas**.

4   From La Caldera to Aguamansa

Popular circuit walk in the pine forests of the upper Orotava Valley

La Caldera – Choza El Topo – Choza Inge Jua – Choza Perez Ventoso – Aguamansa (– La Caldera)

Location: Aguamansa, 1000 m.

Starting point: Zona recreativa La Caldera, 1200 m (picnic area, last bus stop for line 345).

Destination: Aguamansa, 1000 m, bus stop for line 345.

Walking times: La Caldera – Choza El Topo not quite 1 hr, Choza El Topo – Perez Ventoso not quite ½ hr, Perez Ventoso – Aguamansa ½ hr; total time 1¾ hrs.

Ascent: 100 m and 250 m in descent.

Grade: A mostly pleasant walk on forestry roads and streets.

Refreshment: Bar/restaurant at the picnic area La Caldera, bar/restaurants in Aguamansa.

Alternative: From the bus stop in Aguamansa back to the picnic area La Caldera (about 25 min): Walk 50 m uphill along the main road then turn right on the ascending lane that leads along the fence of the trout hatchery. Just before it ends in front of a gate, a *camino* turns off to the left (sign »La Caldera«) then branches after

30 m; go right here. After 10 min, the path merges into a dirt road – turn left here, cross the main road and continue 100 m on the access road in the direction of La Caldera to a signposted walking trail on the right leading up to the picnic area.

Combination possible with Walk 2.

This short circuit route through the splendid pine forests of the upper Orotava Valley is surely a »must« for every Tenerife holidaymaker. The walking path leads from the La Caldera picnic grounds, nestled in a natural crater, past the Órganos rock formations and then down to Aguamansa. A visit to the trout hatchery there is worthwhile.

From the bus stop at the picnic area **La Caldera**, follow the left road past the restaurant and after 2 min turn left onto a wide forestry road (sign »*Los Órganos*«). After 10 min reach a major trail junction next to Choza Pedro Gil (shelter; water available; the *Camino a Candelaria* branches off here to the right). Remain on the forestry road and 5 min later pass under the Los Órganos rock formations – erosion has virtually sculptured »organ pipes« into this massive rock wall. Enjoying the partial shade cast by mighty pines, the wide dirt road now leads through the Barranco de la Madre and passes a large waterworks there 20 m before the *barranco* bridge (a total of 35 min).

After the walk, you can visit the trout hatchery.

A good 5 min later, ignore a forest trail branching off to the left. From time to time, catch some fleeting but beautiful views of Teide and the Orotava Valley – on the coast, we can make out Puerto de la Cruz and when visibility permits, can even see the neighbouring island of La Palma in the distance. After a total of an hour reach **Choza El Topo** (shelter).

Directly past the shelter, a forestry trail branches off to the left, descending in zigzags through the pine and scrub wood. After a good 5 min, the trail forks – go straight (the fork to the right) continuing downhill. Not quite 10 min later reach a trail junction at **Choza Inge Jua** and head to the left steeply downhill. A few minutes later, at the *Choza Perez Ventoso* stone column, the trail merges into a lane ending here. Now continue the descent along this lane, passing between two houses and through fields. At the fork (shrine) 5 min later bear left uphill (to the right leads to La Florida, →Walk 2); a few minutes later at the next fork in the road, turn right. The lane then crosses two *barrancos* and finally merges with the steep village street of **Aguamansa**, onto which we turn left and ascend to the bus stop on the main road. The trout hatchery is located about 200 m further up on the main road.

5 Órganos Trail

Spectacular circuit route around the »Organ Pipes«

La Caldera – Choza El Topo – Órganos Trail – La Caldera

Location: Aguamansa, 1000 m.
Starting point: Zona recreativa La Caldera, 1200 m (picnic area, last bus stop for line 345).
Walking times: La Caldera – Órganos Trail not quite 1¾ hrs, Órganos Trail a good 1½ hrs, descent to La Caldera not quite ¾ hr; total time 4 hrs.
Ascent: A total of 450 m.
Grade: Initially, a pleasant walk on a forestry trail, later, the trail is often steep and slippery and also exposed for a short stretch.
Refreshment: Bar/restaurant at the La Caldera picnic area.

This untamed and idyllic mountain trail offers a diversity of alpine delights – at times even spectacular: the walk passes through the heart of a gorge and crag wonderland above the renowned »Organ Pipes« opening up enchanting views of the Orotava Valley and Teide.

Starting at the car park and bus line terminus at the **La Caldera** picnic area, follow the street to the left past the restaurant and 2 min later, bear left onto a wide forestry road (sign: »*Los Órganos*«). Follow this road straight on, passing Choza Pedro Gil (not quite 10 min; do not turn right) and the Organ Pipes. After a good half hour, pass a large waterworks in Barranco Madre del Agua.

A good 5 min later, 10 m past a forestry trail that forks to the left towards Aguamansa, take a sharp right onto a hiking trail (alternatively, continue on the forestry trail: after a good 20 min, next to Choza El Topo, turn right on the ascending forestry road; some minutes later ignore a left turn; 5 min later in the first left bend ignore the forestry trail turning to the left). Our trail ascends in zigzags along a ridge at the edge of the Barranco Madre del Agua and after just less than a quarter hour meets the forestry road leading to Choza El Topo. In the left bend 10 m on (a forest trail also forks off here to the right) the route continues along the footpath to the right. A good quarter hour later (at a left bend), the footpath merges back into the forestry road which we use to continue our ascent. 10 min later, after the next left bend, the forestry road levels out and leads on the level onto a mountain ridge. After a few minutes, pay close attention: just as the forest trail begins a light ascent, a distinct trail forks to the right at a cairn. The trail leads sometimes steeply along the mountain

The »Organ Pipes« above Aguamansa.

ridge and, after a good 15 min, reaches an **overlook** (about 1670 m) perched on a rocky mountain spur presenting views of Teide and the Orotava Valley. The route continues bearing to the right and 10 m on reaches the crossing of the *Órganos Mountain Trail* which we take to the right (to the left – a delightful excursion possible to Lomo de la Resbala, a good 1½ hrs there and back). Spongy pine needles and easy walking, practically on the level, make this stretch toward Teide a real pleasure. After a short zigzag descent into the Barranco Madre del Agua (20 min), the route continues on easily. 25 min later, a prominent crag comes into view in front of us – Roque Guanchijo. The trail descends once more in zigzags and passes a craggy overlook (25 min). We cross now over the Barranco Las Aguas (10 min) – here the trail is somewhat precipitous, especially along a stretch which leads over a rock ledge skirting around a steep crag (railings on the crag). Immediately after, reach a rocky ridge (with overlook, 10 min). A good 10 min later we pass what is perhaps the finest overlook of the walk: a narrow, jutting ridge of rock. Not quite half an hour later, after a last stretch of steep up-and-down walking leading out of a *barranco*, reach the *Camino a Candelaria* and descend along this to the right. 10 min later cross over a forestry trail (stone column *Lomo de los Brezos*) and continue the descent along the washed-out trail which merges 10 min later by Chozo Pedro Gil with the forestry road that we used on our approach. Take this to the left and return to the **La Caldera** picnic area in 10 min.

6 Choza Chimoche, 1425 m

A ramble in the upper Orotava Valley

Aguamansa – La Caldera – Galería Chimoche – Choza Chimoche – Pedro Gil – La Caldera

Location: Aguamansa, 1000 m.
Starting point: Trout hatchery, 1070 m, on the hairpin bend above Aguamansa (car park for walkers; bus stop for line 345).
Destination: Zona recreativa La Caldera, 1200 m (picnic area with playground and barbecue sites, last bus stop for line 345).
Walking times: Aguamansa – La Caldera ½ hr, La Caldera – Choza Chimoche ¾ hr, Choza Chimoche – La Caldera ¾ hr; total time 2 hrs.
Ascent: About 400 m and 250 m in descent.
Grade: Mostly pleasant walk on forestry and walking trails.
Refreshment: Bar/restaurant at the La Caldera picnic area, in Aguamansa

several bar/restaurants.
Combination possible with Walks 2–8.

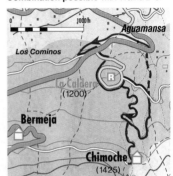

The densely forested upper Orotava Valley is one of the most water-blessed regions on the entire island. On excursions through the thickly-wooded area, walkers will often find mining tunnels (*galerías*) carved deep into the mountain, heaps of rubble as well as pipelines.

Begin on the wide trail passing the trout pools and leave the confines of the **trout hatchery** through a gate in the wall. The path now leads straight on past an aviary with ravens and birds of prey. Shortly after, pass through a large gate and reach a lane that we follow uphill to the left. This ends 200 m on at a gate; before the gate, a *camino* branches off to the left (sign »La Caldera«) and forks after 30 m – turn to the right here. After 10 min, walking straight ahead, the trail merges with a dirt road – turn left here, cross the main road and continue about 100 m on the access road in the direction of **La Caldera** until reaching a signposted walking trail ascending to the right to the picnic area (10 min). A large recreation area with barbecue sites and a playground has been set up at the floor of the crater.

Walk along the dirt road to the right around the picnic area until after a few minutes a slightly ascending forestry road branches off to the right at the highest point of the road (sign »Zona de acampada«). After 200 m, this passes by a campsite then continues almost on the level. After 5 min, ascend gently – soon we can see the Órganos rock formations on the left. About 25 min after the picnic area reach an intersection at the stone column *Pasada de las Bestias*; turn right here and continue on the forestry road. A few minutes later, pass the **Galería Chimoche** – the barred entrance to the water tunnel is located in the valley basin to the right behind the buildings. The dirt road now leads somewhat steeper uphill and after 15 min reaches the shelter of **Choza Chimoche**, 1425 m – here, find an intersecting dirt road which leads to Choza Bermeja to the right (½ hr) and to the Camino a Candelaria to the left; above, a trail continues on to Montaña del Limón (→Walk 7).

Now turn back to the crossing at the stone column *Pasada de las Bestias* (20 min). Here turn to the right onto the gently descending dirt road. After 5 min reach the stone column *Lomo de los Brezos* (Pedro Gil, a pretty vista point 100 m further on), here turn left onto the *Camino a Candelaria* and continue along a zigzag descent. A good 5 min later, after passing the Tres Cruzes (Three Crosses), next to **Choza Pedro Gil** the *camino* merges with a dirt road that (to the left) leads back to the **La Caldera** picnic area in a good 10 min. If you wish to return to Aguamansa, follow the dirt road for not quite 5 min to a bridge. 50 m after the bridge, a wide trail forks off to the right leading straight on in bends back to the trout hatchery (15 min).

The La Caldera picnic area has been set up in a natural crater.

7 Montaña del Limón, 2101 m

Long but varied forest walk with »summit joy«

La Caldera – Montaña del Limón – Choza Chimoche – La Caldera

Location: Aguamansa, 1000 m.
Starting point: Zona recreativa La Caldera, 1200 m (picnic area, last bus stop for line 345).
Walking times: La Caldera – Choza Chimoche turn-off a good ¾ hr, turn-off – Montaña del Limón almost 2 hrs, descent a good 2 hrs; total time 5 hrs.
Ascent: Over 900 m.
Grade: Partially steep walk along forestry and walking trails.
Refreshment: Bar/restaurant at the La Caldera picnic area.
Alternative: Further ascent along the dirt road via Choza J. Ruíz José to Cumbre Dorsal (Corral del Niño, about 1½ hrs); here, follow the road either to the left to the observatories of Izaña (after 10 min turn right) or to the right to El Portillo (almost 1 hr, bus stop for line 348).

The cinder cone of Montaña del Limón rises at the foot of the Cumbre Dorsal from the forest belt of the upper Orotava Valley – often covered in trade wind clouds – and is among the most beautiful panoramic vista points in Tenerife's north.

From the bus stop at the **La Caldera** picnic area, follow the road to the right and after 150 m turn onto the first forestry trail branching off to the right (sign »*Camino de los Guanches*«). 200 m on, the forestry trail swerves to the left – at this point, the old *camino* continues straight ahead, slightly to the left and uphill (sign »Sendero«). At first, the ascent is easy, then climbs more steeply through the thickly-wooded slope and after 10 min crosses a large conduit to the left. About 20 min later, the now not-quite-so-steep *camino* turns to the left toward the slope and 5 min later merges with a forestry road. Follow this 10 m to the right and then sharply to the left, on a distinct trail lined with stones. This leads in gentle up-and-down walking above

The observatories of Izaña are located above Montaña del Limón.

the forestry road through a pine wood, and forks after a good 5 min (35 m after a pile of stones, almost 2 metres high, to the right and above the path).

To the left, a trail leads down to the nearby **Choza Chimoche**, 1425 m (our subsequent return route) – remain to the right on the trail which soon becomes a wide, steep forestry trail. Keeping to the main trail, cross a forestry road in a good half hour at the stone column *Pasada del Faile* (barrier). Continue ascending on the steep forestry trail and after 15 min turn right following the main trail and then 5 min later, meet a forestry road (stone column *Cuevitas de Limón*). Follow this road to the left, easily ascending. After almost 15 min, ignore a forestry trail branching off to the right at a sharp left bend. A good 20 min later, pass the stone column *Cumbrita Fría*. Here, a wide trail of coarse sand branches off to the left between two stone columns and ascends in zigzags through a slope of volcanic debris. After almost half an hour of ascent reach a wide saddle where the trace of a path climbs to the left in 5 min to the highest point of **Montaña del Limón**. From the summit, enjoy a wonderful view of Teide and Cumbre Dorsal with the observatories of Izaña. The secondary peak to the north (10 min) provides a superb downwards view of the Orotava Valley.

Now return to the fork in the trail near **Choza Chimoche** (1½ hrs), here descend to the right and in some minutes reach a forestry road and the shelter. Bear right here and head immediately towards the forestry road branching off to the left. Some minutes later, before a sharp left bend, a distinct path lined with stones branches off and heads straight on, running parallel to the forestry road then merges with it again 10 min later at the stone column *Pasada de las Bestias*. Turn left here, always following the straight forestry road and return to the **La Caldera** picnic area (20 min).

8 Candelaria Trail I
Aguamansa – Montaña de la Crucita, 2057 m

Ascent from the upper Orotava Valley to Cumbre Dorsal

Aguamansa – Choza Pedro Gil – Montaña de la Crucita and back

Location: Aguamansa, 1000 m.
Starting point: Trout hatchery, 1070 m, on the hairpin bend above Aguamansa (car park for walkers; bus stop for line 345).
Walking times: Aguamansa – Choza Pedro Gil 20 min, Choza Pedro Gil – road on the Cumbre Dorsal 2 hrs, descent 1¾ hrs; total time a good 4 hrs.
Ascent: 1000 m.
Grade: Strenuous ascent on a sometimes steep, washed-out *camino*.
Refreshment: Bar/restaurants in Aguamansa.
Alternative: Descent from Mirador La Crucita to Arafo (not quite 3 hrs, →Walk 9): From the *mirador*, a dirt road forks off to the right then 200 m on, a *camino* forks off to the left. The *camino* crosses over the dirt road several times and finally merges with it at the foot of the jet-black cinder cone of Montaña de las Arenas (1 hr). On the dirt road, skirt left around the cinder cone, descending to a stone shelter (½ hr) and in the following right-hand bend, head

straight on, descending further on the *camino*. Continuing straight on (at the fork 100 m before a watercourse, straight on) reach an asphalt road (¾ hr) then bear left at a fork descending steeply to reach Arafo (½ hr, bus stop for line 121).

The Candelaria Trail is an old pilgrim trail which connects Aguamansa with Candelaria – every year on August 14, countless Tinerfeños make a pilgrimage here for the festival of the archipelago's patron saint. The beauty of the upper Orotava Valley is revealed in all it's splendour: through the vast pine forests above Aguamansa and over volcanic slopes shimmering in every shade of red, the trail ascends to the ridgeline of Cumbre Dorsal which offers a spectacular view of the Orotava Valley to the west and the Güímar Valley to the east. If you wish, you can walk the entire length of the Candelaria Trail to Arafo.

At the hairpin bend at the **trout hatchery** of Aguamansa, the signposted *Camino a Candelaria* begins, ascending in a leisurely fashion through a wood of heather trees and pines. After a good 5 min, the *camino* merges with a forestry trail that leads to the left to a forester's house. Walk to the left past the house and immediately after continue ascending by turning right onto the

View of the Orotava Valley from the walking trail with La Palma in the background.

camino. Directly afterwards, cross a forestry trail (on the right is the Galería La Puente). Now either continue straight ahead ascending along the track or – a prettier choice – after 10 m fork to the left onto a trail flanked by stones that ascends over a ridge skirting the Barranco de Los Llanos, with a sublime view of the Órganos Pipes. Not quite 10 min later, the two trails come together again and merge with a forestry road coming from the La Caldera picnic area. Follow this 20 m to the left then, to the right of **Choza Pedro Gil**, change over to the old *camino* (sign »*Camino a Candelaria*«).

The steep zigzag trail passes Tres Cruzes (Three Crosses) and then, after a quarter hour at the stone column *Lomo de los Brezos* (Pedro Gil) crosses over a forestry road – bearing to the left, the ascent continues steeply. After 10 min, a descending trail branches off to the right; here continue the ascent straight on. 5 min later, the Órganos Trail merges from the left (→Walk 5). 50 m later, take a left fork (do not continue straight on the wide trail to Choza Chimoche traversing the slope; shortly afterwards take a right fork to remain on the main trail). The *camino* continues a steep, zigzag ascent. A half hour later, the pine forest begins to thin out – opening up a view of the Orotava Valley and the coast. Past a lava flow, a stretch passes through a colourful, mostly dark-red, volcanic terrain. Another half hour later – now traversing in a north-easterly direction – climb over a lava flow. Unfortunately, the traverse soon ends, then the steeper ascent continues over a craggy outcropping to the ridgeline road of the Cumbre Dorsal which we reach 30 m before **Mirador La Crucita**, 1980 m (halfway along this stretch, a path forks left away from the main road and ascends in 10 min to the highest point of **Montaña de la Crucita**).

9 Candelaria Trail II
Arafo – Montaña de la Crucita, 2057 m

Magnificent walk through vineyards, pine and chestnut woods and an impressive mountain landscape – one of the most beautiful walks of the island!

Arafo – Montaña de las Arenas – Montaña de la Crucita and back

Starting point: Church square in the town centre of Arafo, 463 m (bus stop for line 121).
Walking times: Arafo – Montaña de las Arenas 2¼ hrs, Montaña de las Arenas – road on Cumbre Dorsal 1½ hrs, descent 3 hrs; total time 6¾ hrs.
Ascent: 1600 m.
Grade: Strenuous, extremely diverse day

hike on a sometimes steep *camino*.
Refreshment: Bars and restaurants in Arafo.
Alternatives: Ascent of Montaña de las Arenas via the dirt road by the barrier (almost ¼ hr one way, no distinct trail; excellent 360° view!). Possible descent from Montaña de la Crucita to Aguamansa (→Walk 8).

Due to its diverse scenery, the strenuous ascent from Arafo to Montaña de la Crucita is one of the most beautiful routes on Tenerife. Especially impressive in the higher stretches – the unique setting of black sand and dark-red lava slopes with pine woods shimmering in bright green and rocky mountains stretching to the heavens.

Directly above the church, perches the village square of **Arafo**; a kiosk pavilion is located in its centre. Walk past this and continue straight on ascending the *Calle General Franco*; at a small square, this becomes the *Calle de Eduardo Curbelo Fariña*. The street now steepens and soon leaves the last houses of Arafo behind. At first, ignore streets branching off but after a total of a good quarter hour turn left at an intersection and immediately (15 m on) begin ascending again through vineyards, orchards and terraces planted with potatoes. 20 min later the street comes to an end but a trail continues on, opening lovely views of the Güímar Valley as it ascends.

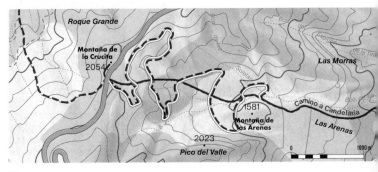

Uniquely breathtaking scenery – we have a view over the mountain valley with the black slag cone of the Montaña de las Arenas down to the coast near Güímar.

Soon the route passes between two waterworks sheds – here a watercourse joins us along the trail's edge. The stone-paved *camino* now enters a sunny pine wood and not quite 10 min later diverts to the left from the watercourse to begin a zigzag ascent (ignore the left fork; a few minutes later ignore the right fork that crosses over the watercourse). From time to time, we can discover small red markings along the trail. The ascending trail, cushioned by spongy needles, is mostly pleasant. About 25 min from the asphalt road, cross an open, usually dry watercourse. The *camino* now leads to the left into a pine wood and then ascends in zigzags. After a good half hour, having left the wood shortly before, and passing through rock rose undergrowth, reach a small **stone shelter** at a dirt road – surrounded by gnarled and bent chestnut trees, in whose shade there are pretty resting spots with a view of the southern coast between Puertito de Güímar and Candelaria; we can even make

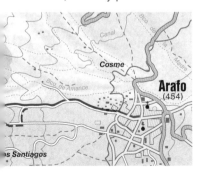

out Teresitas Beach and the neighbouring island of Gran Canaria.

Past the stone shelter, continue the steep ascent on the sandy road. Chestnut trees are still in evidence for a short time longer, then the black volcanic cone of Montaña de las Arenas gets closer and closer. The track leads in a left-hand bend skirting to the right of the foot of this beautifully-shaped volcano (you can also take a shortcut straight on along the steep track) then passes a barrier. A good 100 m on, a distinct sand trail branches off straight ahead at a right-hand bend (10 m after passing a track forking to the left) offering a shortcut to avoid the wide bend made by the dirt road. On the dirt road again, enter a broad, mostly wooded mountain valley that opens up beyond **Montaña de las Arenas**, 1589 m. To the south, the valley ends at the mighty rock cliffs of Pico del Valle, 2023 m, and to the north-east, at equally impressive mountains; to the west, the valley stretches up to the ridgeline of Cumbre Dorsal with Montaña de la Crucita, 2057 m.

After a good 100 m, in the following left bend, leave the dirt road along a gently ascending path diagonally to the right – walkers wishing to turn back here should find a suitable resting spot further along the road in the pine wood. Our *camino* now leads into the pine wood, easily crossing the slope and ascends for a short time through a small, treeless *barranco* then continues the ascent

A blanket of needles and lava chips provide a soft walking surface.

Shrine on the side of the pilgrimage trail.

to the left in zigzags through the pine wood. A quarter hour after leaving the dirt road, we cross over it again and continue along the small trail. A good 5 min later, cross the dirt road again and 10 min later, once again (to the left, above the next bend in the dirt road, we see layers of rock shimmering in a range of colours, from red to black): take the track 15 m to the right until joining the *camino* which continues on to the left; this climbs a mountain ridge and opens up a fantastic panorama of the entire mountain valley, then the pine wood once again surrounds us. The trail now becomes a bit steeper. About 20 min later the wood thins out – we are now ascending through red volcanic debris. This panoramic section along toilsome, sandy ground is the most strenuous part of the hike. Soon pass a tiny shrine then cross the dirt road once again – a few metres on to the left, the *camino* continues. Now it takes only another 10 min (above on the dirt road to the right) to reach the mountain road which follows the Cumbre Dorsal ridge next to **Mirador La Crucita**, 1980 m. 30 m farther to the left and on the other side of the ridge, the Candelaria Trail leads to Aguamansa – midway along this stretch, you can turn right onto a steep footpath and climb in 10 min to the highest point of **Montaña de la Crucita**; although somewhat blocked by pines, enjoy a spectacular view of the Orotava Valley, Teide and the Güímar Valley.

10 Ladera de Güímar

Magnificent panoramic and *galería* walk above the Güímar Valley

Güímar – Las Coloradas – Canal de Fasnia – Barranco del Agua – Barranco Tegüigo – Ladera de Güímar and back

Starting point: Güímar, 289 m, parish church San Pedro at the upper end of the town square (bus stop for lines 120, 121 and 127). Those approaching by car can drive up to the end of the asphalt road (note on access: take a left at the intersection above the San Pedro church, then a right at the traffic circle; continue as described below; very steep!).

Walking times: Güímar – end of asphalt road 1¼ hrs, further on to the watercourse a good ½ hr, watercourse walk 1 hr, return route 2½ hrs; total time 5 hrs (or 3 hrs from end of asphalt road).

Ascent: About 700 m.

Grade: To the watercourse, an easy, although sometimes steep ascent on an asphalt/dirt road. The continued route on the covered watercourse starts out somewhat overgrown (some of the cover plates are damaged!). A powerful torch is necessary for traversing the tunnels (very dark, two tunnels about 10 min).

Refreshment: Bar/restaurants in Güímar.

Adventurers will surely get their money's worth on this walk. After a strenuous ascent through cultivated terraces and pine woods, a panoramic mountain hike awaits us along a sometimes-covered watercourse which ultimately brings us through two long tunnels and finally to the steep precipice of the Ladera de Güímar. A powerful torch is absolutely necessary for some stretches along the low and narrow tunnels.

In **Güímar**, take the pedestrian street to the left of the San Pedro church up to the intersection above the church. Here head diagonally to the left onto a village street (*Calle San Pedro Arriba*) continuing uphill. After 5 min, turn left at house no. 88 onto a lane (sign »*Barrio de La Hoya*«) which immediately crosses a *barranco*. The lane passes a church and then forks 100 m later – continue straight on along the street, easily at first, before ascending sometimes steeply through cultivated terraces. After a total of 1¼ hrs reach

The galería at the end of the walk along the watercourse.

the forest's edge, the street now becoming a bumpy dirt road (parking possible).

Not quite 10 min later, the dirt road forks; bear to the left to continue the ascent (pay attention here for the return!). Pass through a dense scrub wood of rock rose, heather, laurel and strawberry trees. After almost half an hour, directly past a turnabout, a steep, bumpy dirt road branches off to the left and after just 5 min ends at the **Canal de Fasia** and a pile of canal cover plates.

Now follow the covered watercourse to the left – a beautiful mountain trail at a good 1000 m in altitude, leading almost on the level through sparse pine forest (sometimes somewhat overgrown at the start) and opening a marvellous view of the Güímar Valley and of Gran Canaria. After half an hour, cross the **Barranco del Agua** then pass through a short tunnel to only enter yet another tunnel. Traversing this tunnel takes a good 10 min along the maintenance path beside the watercourse and requires a lot of stooping and ducking (watch for rocks sticking out of the ceiling). Suddenly, we are standing before the deep sheer-faced gorge of the **Barranco Tegüigo**.

Now continue to the right, over the large conduit and reach another, overgrown tunnel opening. The watercourse is dry here so you can also walk in the channel itself (caution: tiny dams underfoot!). After almost 10 min, the tunnel merges in a gallery corridor with a channel. We are now directly across from the steeply protruding rock wall of **Ladera de Güímar**. The left branch of the gallery corridor then ends, but you really should walk for a short distance to the right until the channel exits the gallery corridor (caution: falling rock!) because from there, you can enjoy a fantastic view in the direction of Güímar. You also have the option of walking about 20 min more to reach another small *barranco* cleft.

11 From Aguamansa to Mirador La Corona via Chanajiga

Quiet forest walk straight through the upper Orotava Valley

Aguamansa – Cruz de Luis – Chanajiga – Mirador La Corona – Icod el Alto

Location: Aguamansa, 1000 m.
Starting point: Trout hatchery at the hairpin bend above Aguamansa, 1070 m (bus stop for line 345).
Destination: Bar/restaurant »Mirador El Lance« in Icod el Alto, 560 m (bus stop for line 354).
Walking times: Aguamansa – Galería Pino Soler 1 hr, Galería Pino Soler – Choza Cruz de Luis 1¼ hrs, Choza Cruz

de Luis – Chanajiga ¼ hr, Chanajiga – Mirador La Corona 1¾ hrs, Mirador La Corona – Icod el Alto ½ hr; total time 4¾ hrs.
Ascent: Almost 200 m and 700 m in descent.
Grade: Not counting the descent to Icod el Alto, a pleasant but long walk on forestry roads.
Refreshment: Bars and restaurants in Aguamansa and in Icod el Alto.

Walkers who are not drawn to adventurous and strenuous mountain hiking will be pleased by this walk along the timberline of the upper Orotava Valley. It leads from Aguamansa to the Chanajiga picnic area, over the western cliff face with the fabulous vista point »La Corona« and down to Icod el Alto. Along the way, there are opportunities for descents to Benijos, Las Llanadas, and Palo Blanco (bus stops for line 347).

Walk along the wide trail past the trout pools and leave the **trout hatchery** on the trail passing through a gate in the wall. The trail now leads straight on past an aviary. Shortly after, pass through a large gate and reach a lane; follow this to the left until it ends 200 m later at another gate. Before reaching this gate, a *camino* branches off to the left (sign »La Caldera«) then forks 30 m on – here, go to the right. 10 min later and always straight on, the trail merges with a dirt road (sign »Pista de Benijos«) near the main road at the turn-off which leads to the La Caldera picnic area.

Follow the dirt road to the right, always straight on. After 15 min, a short path branches off to the right to Galería La Fortuita; 15 min later, bear to the left at a fork (sign »A Los

Realejos«). The dirt road now crosses through the Barranco Siete and shortly after, the Barranco de la Suerte with **Galería Pino Soler**.

A few minutes later, bear left at a fork (sign »A Los Realejos«; the right fork leads to Choza Antonio Lugo, not far away, and from there a descent is possible to Benijos, ½ hr). Head straight on and almost 10 min later pass the stone column *Morro Quemado* (to the left, a possible ascent to the main road with the Choza Wildpret, ¾ hr). 10 min later, reach another stone column *Lomo de los Tomillos*. The dirt road continues straight on, passes the stone columns *Salto Bangarro* (bear right at the fork) and *Lomo Alto* (straight on; 15 min later, at two successive forks, bear left) then reach **Choza Cruz de Luis** at a major trail junction after a walk totalling 40 min. Here continue by passing to the right of the shelter. After a good 10 min, the dirt road merges into a road ascending from Las Llanadas (to the right, a possible descent to Palo Blanco/Realejo Alto via a *camino* that forks away from the road on the first bend to the right. Continuing straight on, soon reach the large **Chanajiga** picnic area (barbecue and picnic sites).

Passing the playground of the picnic area, the dirt road continues. It leads almost on the level into Ladera de Tigaiga, the western cliff face of the Orotava Valley which opens a beautiful view of the broad valley gently dropping towards the ocean. After about 10 min, pass Mirador de Sergio (sign). Almost 1 hr after the picnic area, reach a major junction of dirt roads on the ridgeline of the *ladera* (stone column *Corral Quemado*). Somewhat below, we can already see Mirador de Asomados (radio tower). Now follow the track branching off to the right that descends passing the *mirador* on the left. The steep track often crosses or brushes past a dirt road ascending from Mirador La Corona. After 45 min, reach the overlook pavilion at **Mirador La Corona** (to the right, a possible descent via the *camino* to the main road between Realejo Alto and Icod El Alto; bus stop for line 354).

From here, descend farther along a dirt trail in a westerly direction which finally merges into an asphalt street to reach the village **Icod el Alto** and then the main road between Los Realejos and La Guancha. Here, turn right and after 150 m finish the walk at the overlook and bar/restaurant »Mirador El Lance«.

45

12 From Mirador La Corona to El Portillo

Strenuous, panoramic ascent over the Ladera de Tigaiga

Icod el Alto – Mirador La Corona – Choza Viera y Clavijo – Choza Piedra de los Pastores – Cruz de Fregel – Roque del Peral – El Portillo

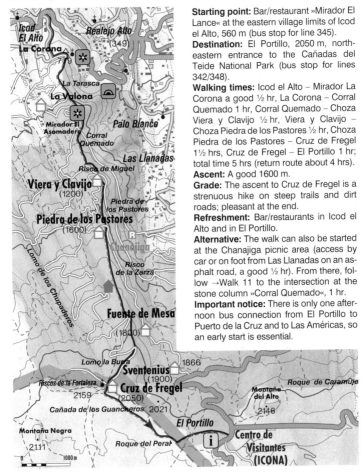

Starting point: Bar/restaurant »Mirador El Lance« at the eastern village limits of Icod el Alto, 560 m (bus stop for line 345).

Destination: El Portillo, 2050 m, north-eastern entrance to the Cañadas del Teide National Park (bus stop for lines 342/348).

Walking times: Icod el Alto – Mirador La Corona a good ½ hr, La Corona – Corral Quemado 1 hr, Corral Quemado – Choza Viera y Clavijo ½ hr, Viera y Clavijo – Choza Piedra de los Pastores ½ hr, Choza Piedra de los Pastores – Cruz de Fregel 1½ hrs, Cruz de Fregel – El Portillo 1 hr; total time 5 hrs (return route about 4 hrs).

Ascent: A good 1600 m.

Grade: The ascent to Cruz de Fregel is a strenuous hike on steep trails and dirt roads; pleasant at the end.

Refreshment: Bar/restaurants in Icod el Alto and in El Portillo.

Alternative: The walk can also be started at the Chanajiga picnic area (access by car or on foot from Las Llanadas on an asphalt road, a good ½ hr). From there, follow →Walk 11 to the intersection at the stone column »Corral Quemado«, 1 hr.

Important notice: There is only one afternoon bus connection from El Portillo to Puerto de la Cruz and to Las Américas, so an early start is essential.

What a walk! – constantly close to the edge of the western cliff face of the Orotava Valley, this panoramic walk climbs up into the uniquely beautiful »lunar landscape« of the Cañadas. The ascent is extremely strenuous but hikers are rewarded with an absolutely magnificent view of Teide and Montaña Blanca.

From Mirador El Lance at the village limits of **Icod el Alto** ascend 150 m along the main road then at the left-hand bend make a turn to the left onto the *Carretera Transversal 1 El Lance*. After about 200 m, a steeply ascending village street forks sharply to the right; always use this to continue the ascent. After a good 15 min, an asphalted/cemented track forks to the left and at the same time passes a house. Reaching an-

Pavilion at the Mirador La Corona.

other house, the track becomes a dirt trail which ascends directly to **Mirador La Corona**; the radio towers there can already be seen. From the vista pavilion, enjoy an incredible downward view of the Orotava Valley.

A track passes to the left of the former bar/restaurant then climbs along the Orotava Valley's cliff's edge and through terraces. After a good 10 min, cross a track (to the left – some radio towers) and enter a scrub wood; scrub woods predominate the landscape at this elevation. Not quite 10 min later, reach a trail junction. Continue a steep ascent along the middle track; this can be extremely slippery when wet. At the next junction (a good 5 min) continue the ascent by bearing left. 40 min after leaving La Corona, pass the last radio towers on the western cliff face (Mirador de Asomados). Subsequently, the steep track often crosses over the dirt forestry road that ascends in long, drawn-out bends (always continue along the cliff's edge; at the end, along a footpath). After a good quarter hour, reach a major junction of dirt roads and a stone column (*Corral Quemado*) – to the left, a forestry road leads to the Chanajiga picnic area (→Walk 11, 1 hr), bearing right, a forestry road ascends towards La Guancha (→Walk 13), straight on (25 m to the right, then sharply left) a dirt road continues towards El Portillo. Remain on the wide main dirt road and after almost half an hour reach the stone shelter **Choza Viera y Clavijo**, 1200 m.

To the left, a detour can be made to an overlook with a view of the Orotava Valley, but we turn to the right towards the main junction then bear to the left

The ascent to Mirador La Corona – backwards view of Icod El Alto

along the ascending dirt road (sign »Cañadas«). At forks in the trail, always bear left continuing along the dirt road until reaching **Choza Piedra de los Pastores** after half an hour (100 m before reaching this point, a lovely trail forks to the left to the Chanajiga picnic area, a rewarding variant for hikers preferring the circuit walk La Corona – Piedra de los Pastores – Chanajiga – Corral Quemado – La Corona instead of the continued ascent to El Portillo). The view of the Orotava Valley is fantastic; beneath us, we can make out the Chanajiga picnic area at the edge of the timberline.

To the left, a dirt forestry road continues in the direction of Cañadas – but we follow the forestry road which ascends straight on over the high ridge, continuing directly towards Teide which appears just in front of us. Some minutes later, pass a shrine. A good quarter hour later, the forestry road noticeably levels out and after a few minutes reaches a fork – here bear left, continuing the ascent over a treeless fire-break. Suddenly, the pine forest disappears behind us – we now have a full view of Teide in its titanic entirety, as well as of the Fortaleza ridge. Teide broom lines the way and off the road to the right, a forestry house appears. Almost an hour after Choza Piedra de los Pastores, the trail merges with an ascending dirt forestry road coming from the right, which we take but then leave immediately at the next bend onto the track branching off to the left. After 10 min meet up with the dirt road again and follow this to the left, but in the next bend, walk out a little further to the left to enjoy a wonderful view of the Orotava Valley: the boundless panorama stretches from the coast over vast expanses of forest to the Cumbre Dorsal – weather permitting, of course. The dirt road now runs almost on the level toward the Degollada del Cedro, the saddle between the ochre-coloured Fortaleza ridge and the Cabezón. After a quarter hour, a bumpy dirt road joins us from the right, and then we can see the small chapel in front of us and the shelter on the saddle at **Cruz de Fregel**, 2084 m. Several benches and tables supply a resting place under shady pines.

If you wish, you can take a side trip to the summit plateau of Risco de la Fortaleza (→Walk 43), however, we climb down the path (between the two tracks) along the other side of the saddle and into the light-coloured sandy plain of **Cañada de los Guancheros**; here, bear to the left. At the end of the plain, a distinct trail continues which ascends for a short distance and then leads in gentle up-and-down walking to the foot of **Roque del Peral** (a good ½ hr). Circumvent the group of crags in a short ascent to the left and 75 m after the hill near the rocky crags, a distinct hiking trail branches off to the left (40 min from Cruz de Fregel). Follow this trail straight on, at the end passing through a gate in a fence (bear right at the next fork) to the national park visitor centre **El Portillo**.

After the long, steep ascent, a comfortable picnic area with a view to Pico del Teide awaits us on Cruz de Fregel.

13 From Mirador La Corona to La Guancha

Extensive forest hike at the northern foot of Pico del Teide

Icod el Alto – Mirador La Corona – Corral Quemado – Barranco de Fuente Pedro – Barranco de la Arena – El Lagar – La Guancha

Starting point: Bar/restaurant »Mirador El Lance« at the eastern village limits of Icod el Alto, 560 m (bus stop for line 354).
Destination: La Guancha, 495 m (bus stop for line 354).
Walking times: Icod el Alto – La Corona a good ½ hr, La Corona – Corral Quemado 1 hr, Corral Quemado – Campamento Bco. de la Arena 2 hrs, Campamento Bco. de la Arena – El Lagar 1 hr, El Lagar – La

Guancha 1¼ hrs; total time 6 hrs.
Ascent: A good 900 m and almost 1000 m in descent.
Grade: A steep ascent to Corral Quemado, then a pleasant forest walk.
Refreshment: Bar/restaurants in Icod el Alto and in La Guancha.
Alternative: Begin the walk at the Chanajiga picnic area. From there, follow →Walk 11 to the junction Corral Quemado, 1 hr.

On this walk, you can experience Teide from its most impressive side: the sheer northern cliffs, often snow-covered in winter, plunge down to the forest belt above La Guancha – an extraordinary sight!

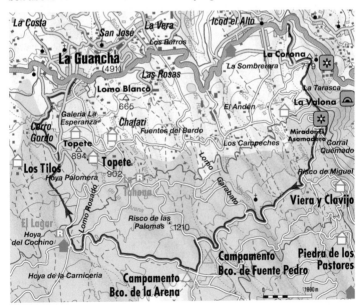

From **Icod el Alto**, as described under →Walk 12, first climb up to the trail junction with the stone column *Corral Quemado* (1½ hrs). Take the ascending dirt road that bears to the right (after 25 m ignore a left fork). After a quarter hour (at the rain gauge) continue straight on (left) then a good 100 m on, bear right at a fork. Subsequently, the forestry road crosses over a *barranco* via a stone bridge and then continues the ascent by bearing left at the fork and, 50 m later, right at a second fork. Continue straight on and after about 20 min pass the stone column *Los Campeches* then cross through the mighty Barranco de la Degollada. At the stone column *Lomo del Astillero* (¼ hr, shrine) once again continue straight on (bearing left) and shortly thereafter to the right (straight on) at the fork. 5 min later, pass the stone column *Barranco de los Charcos* and a good 10 min later, pass the stone column *Lomo de las Piedras* (both times continuing straight on). At the stone column *Caño Chingue* (10 min), on the floor of a small *barranco*, bear left at the fork onto the track toward *Barranco de la Arena* (sign; the forestry road continuing straight on leads to the La Tahona picnic area, ¾ hr). For a short distance, pass through a gorge surrounded by cliffs then the track enters a broad mountain valley. Passing **Campamento Barranco de Fuente Pedro** (barbecue sites) reach a junction of dirt roads after almost a quarter hour (stone column *Barranco de la Arena*; straight on, to Galería Vergara, 25 min; left to El Portillo). Here, take the fork to the right signposted for La Guancha and at the same time reach the holiday grounds of **Aula de Naturaleza Barranco de la Arena** (houses, picnic area). The dirt road passes this to the right (parallel – an old *camino*). After an hour reach an important road junction and then immediately afterward the **El Lagar** picnic area.

From the forestry house, follow the dirt road that descends to the right along the recreation area (after 5 min straight on). Not quite 10 min later at a large lay-by, a distinct sometimes stone-paved *camino* forks to the left from the dirt road, descending along a small ridge. Afterwards, cross over a forestry road three times and, after a total of a good 10 min, reach the forestry road for a fourth time, merging here with the dirt road leading to La Guancha. Across from the merging point (to the right of the dirt road) the *camino* continues. At the fork 30 m on, remain on the main trail by bearing right. Shortly after, in a left bend, a trail merges from the right. Now always bearing slightly to the right, descend along the main trail that crosses the dirt road again not quite 10 min later (10 m right). A good 5 min later, the wide *camino* once again crosses the dirt road (20 m on, descend right) then crosses it again 5 min later. A covered watercourse merges from the left following the edge of the trail. 3 min later, the *camino* once again crosses the road (now asphalt) and then becomes a forestry trail that, 3 min later, we leave turning sharply left onto a cobblestone path. Shortly after, the trail merges with a street, where we turn right to descend to the main road in **La Guancha** (not quite ½ hr, the bus stop is to the right).

14 Volcán Garachico (Montaña Negra), 1401 m

Short excursion into the more recent volcanic history of the island

Las Arenas Negras – Volcán Garachico and back

Location: La Montañeta, 950 m (bus stop for line 360).
Starting point: Zona recreativa Las Arenas Negras, 1250 m (picnic area). Those arriving by bus get off at the stop at the upper end of La Montañeta (Ermita San Francisco). From there, either continue uphill on the main road to the signposted left turn-off of the dirt road to Las Arenas Negras (800 m; a good 10 min) or across from the chapel (stone column »Ermita«) take the path to reach a forestry trail; ascend this to the left and then follow the main road to the left to reach the right-hand turn-off of the dirt road to Las Arenas Negras (20 min). Continue along this for 2.2 km (½ hr) to the picnic area.
Walking times: Las Arenas Negras – stone column almost ¾ hr, return route ½ hr; total time almost 1¼ hrs (ascent from La Montañeta – an additional ¾ hr one way).
Ascent: 200 m.
Grade: Easy walk with a short section lacking a distinct path.
Refreshment: In La Montañeta and San José de los Llanos.
Alternative: Ascent from the stone column El Volcán Negro to the volcano summit of Chinyero (1¼ hrs, return 1 hr): On the other side of the dirt road over the watercourse, a wide trail leads uphill. This branches after a few minutes; go left here and a few minutes later cross a gravel trail where a pretty sand trail continues diagonally to the left and then becomes a path a little later. The path merges with a dirt forestry road (left) which leads straight to a volcanic mountain. A few minutes later, bear left at the turn-off for 20 m until a path branches off to the right marked by a faded blue arrow marking. After some minutes, the path merges with a dirt road.

Take this to the left. After 10 min leave the dirt road and turn right on a scree-covered path that ascends to Chinyero, 1561 m.

Blockhouse on the way to Volcán Garachico (in background).

The Las Arenas Negras picnic area is the most convenient starting point for short excursions into the vast volcano and forest belt north-west of the Teide massif. The contrast between the jet-black slopes of volcanic debris and slag cones with the shimmering bright green of the pine woods is marvellous – a picturesque landscape!

In front of the car park of the **Las Arenas Negras** recreation area in the left-hand bend in the dirt road, a blocked track branches off to the right (sign) and some minutes later leads to a cluster of blockhouses. Straight on, the spur of a trail leads to the Volcán Garachico; this ascent, however, is now prohibited to preserve the natural terrain. Thus, after passing a long blockhouse, turn right at the fork. The trail passes toilet facilities on the right, leads past an area of rubble and then continues along the foot of Volcán Garachico. Almost 10 min from the blockhouses, the trail hooks to the left and then becomes a path which ascends onto a mountain ridge for a short time (to the upper left a survey post). The orange-marked path now leads in easy up-and-down walking through the imposing lava flows that the volcano spewed forth towards Garachico in 1706. Afterwards, the path descends again, leading into a sandy terrain dotted with young pines; cross this area, keeping slightly to the right. After a total of almost 30 min, enter a sparse pine wood by turning left onto a path which is rather indistinct but ascends easily (always bearing slightly to the left). After about 10 min reach an intersecting dirt road that runs directly below the Vergara canal. Now follow this to the left to reach the **stone column El Volcán Negro** at the foot of Volcán Garachico (a good 5 min, turn-off to Chinyero, →Alternative). Remain on the dirt road and turn left some minutes later onto a distinct trail that brings us along the foot of the cinder cone back to the blockhouses and finally to the **Las Arenas Negras** picnic area.

15 Montaña Reventada, 2230 m

Volcano walk at the foot of Pico Viejo

Chío–Boca Tauce road – Montaña Reventada – Montaña de la Botija – Chío–Boca Tauce road

Starting point: Road sign »Montaña Samara« at the southern foot of Montaña Samara, on the Cañadas road from Chío to Boca Tauce between Km 7 and 8.

Walking times: Road – Montaña Reventada 1¼ hrs, Montaña Reventada – Montaña de la Botija ¾ hr, Montaña de la Botija – road ½ hr; total time 2½ hrs.

Ascent: Almost 400 m.

Grade: A mostly pleasant walk along trails and paths. The crater rim of Montaña

Reventada is narrow and precipitous in the upper section – in stormy weather, it is best to postpone the ascent to the summit. Orientation can be a problem during periods of poor visibility.

Alternative: From the starting point, there is also a possible ascent to Montaña Samara, 1937 m – this takes not quite a quarter hour and is easy to follow via a path leading to the right along the ridgeline.

The Montaña Reventada is one of the many cinder cones that emerge from the vast lava landscape at the foot of Pico Viejo. The route to the cone passes several craters and lava flows.

From the road sign »*Montaña Samara*« follow the sand trail heading east towards Teide. This leads parallel to the road at first then diverges away from it. After some minutes, pass between two flat groups of rocks and then a rain gauge to your right (here and at the following fork, continue straight on; do not go left). After a good quarter hour, approach a vast field of lava and skirt around at the edge to the left through coarse volcanic sand. Always staying on the main trail, now ascend through a gully to the right of the black cinder cone of Montaña de la Botija. Behind us, in the distance, we can see the island of Gomera, behind this to the left – El Hierro, and further right, with the double humps, La Palma – before us, the mighty Pico Viejo appears and behind it, the Pan de Azucár juts skyward. The path continues towards these peaks and soon leads along the edge of another vast lava field in a flat valley. Gradually,

At the start of the walking trail – in the foreground: Montaña de la Botija – Pico Viejo and Pico del Teide in the background.

after a total of 50 min, reach the heights of a volcanic sand ridge – to the left and somewhat below, we see a lone young pine. Here, a path marked by a cairn turns sharply off to the left and leads back in the direction of Montaña de la Botija (our subsequent return route), however, we continue straight on along the ridge and toward Montaña Reventada. After 10 min, we find ourselves at the south-west ridge of our summit goal. Over the narrow ridge which is somewhat exposed further up, climb to the highest point of **Montaña Reventada** and from there, enjoy a splendid view of the almost 1000 metre higher Pico Viejo.

The descent initially follows along the ascent route. After about 20 min, branch off to the right onto the path marked with a cairn next to the lone pine and, bearing right, keep along the edge of a rugged lava flow leading down from Montaña Reventada. After almost 10 min, stay to the left on the main path which now diverges further away from the lava flow in a slight ascent and 10 min later reaches a small saddle. Here is a possibility to take a side trip along a path in a good 5 min to **Montaña de la Botija**, 2118 m, with a far-reaching view to the west. Back on the saddle, the path dips slightly, keeping to the left, through the volcanic debris-covered flank of Montaña Botija and then merges again with the ascent route a quarter hour later. On this stretch, we pass the rain gauge after 100 m and then return to the starting point.

The Teno Massif and the South-west

Untamed *barrancos* and sensational coastline cliffs

The Teno Mountains in the extreme north-west of the island offer hikers a wonderful walking terrain – for the most part still in a pristine state. Like the Anaga massif, the Teno massif belongs to the oldest mountain ranges on Tenerife and boasts numerous dramatic gorges – especially to the west along the coastline cliffs, plunging almost vertically to depths of nearly 600 m (»Acantilado de los Gigantes«) – the most famous of these is the Barranco de Masca, one of the classic hiking destinations on the island. Also, in the north, the Teno massif, cut by deep barrancos, drops steeply down to the fertile coast and is blanketed by banana plantations near Buenavista and Los Silos.

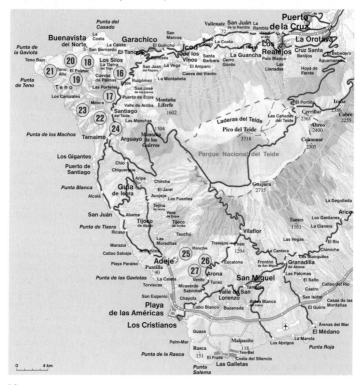

56

Las Portelas in the idyllic Palmar Valley with the Baracán in the background.

The Teno Mountains reach an altitude of about 1000 m and are virtually tree-less with the exception of the slopes on the north-east side where a few dense laurisilva forests are still located – the archaic, often windblown and cloud-covered landscape on the barren Teno plateau seems almost desolate. Palmar Valley and especially Masca Valley, with its picturesque palm groves, are exceptions to the rule.

Towards the south, this region is bordered by the south-west coast, excellently developed for tourism but in some places somewhat spoiled as a result. Los Gigantes and Puerto de Santiago, the sunniest seaside resorts on the island not only boast a wonderful sand beach at Playa de la Arena but are also ideal bases for hikers wishing to limit their walks primarily to the western part of the island; on the other hand, Las Américas, Los Cristianos and the other seaside resorts of the southern coast have the advantage of motorway access to Santa Cruz. The caldera rim mountains slope gently down to the coast on this side, furrowed by sometimes abysmally-deep *barrancos* such as the Barranco del Infierno. In the regions around Adeje, Arona and the Valle de San Lorenzo, there are also a few imposing rocky mountains which present a worthwhile destination for hikers.

16 From Los Silos to Erjos

On old *caminos* through the laurel woods of Monte del Agua

Los Silos – Bco. de Bucarón – Erjos – Bco. de Cuevas Negras – Los Silos

Starting point: Church on the main road in the centre of Los Silos, 109 m (bus stop for lines 107/363/365).

Walking times: Los Silos – crest with dilapidated houses 1 hr, further route to Las Moradas 1 hr, further route to Erjos 1½ hrs, Erjos – Las Cuevas Negras almost 1 hr, Las Cuevas Negras – Los Silos a good ¾ hr; total time 5½ hrs.

Ascent: About 950 m.

Grade: Overall, a strenuous but usually pleasant walk on beautiful old *caminos* and forestry roads.

Refreshment: Bars in Los Silos and in Erjos.

Alternative: From the stone column Las Moradas to Las Portelas: Continue to the right on the forestry road in the direction of »Calabacera« (sign). At a barrier, this merges with a wide dirt road (stone column »La Calabacera«) which leads to Erjos to the left and Las Portelas to the right (staying on the dirt road; 1 hr from Las Moradas, bus stop for lines 355/366).

The laurisilva forests of Monte del Agua above Los Silos are among the most pristine on the island. Beautiful old *caminos* and shady forestry trails open up this densely forested area of the Teno Mountains to the hiker. If the walk from Los Silos to Erjos and back down to Los Silos is too strenuous, you can also begin the hike in Erjos – this shortens the walk by almost two hours but still includes most of the beautiful features of the walk.

A lane to the right leads past the church of **Los Silos** and heads towards the mountains – *Calle Susana*. After about 200 m, at a small bridge, reach the stone column *Los Avadepos* – here, go right on the track along the stream bed. After about 100 m, a path branches off to the left continuing along the

On the descent from Barranco de Cuevas Negras. Los Silos before us.

stream bed and leads along a slight incline to **Barranco de Bucarón**. Here, the path becomes a pretty cobblestone trail which soon crosses a covered watercourse and, a short distance later, crosses a bridge and switches to the left side of the valley. 5 min later, having crossed another watercourse, the *camino* switches back to the right side of the valley which now gradually widens. After a few minutes, the trail branches; here, go right in an uphill sweep, back to the stream bed. Now a few dilapidated stone houses appear on the ridgeline to the left of the valley; the *camino* heads towards these passing through blackberry bushes. From here, enjoy a lovely downwards view into the deep, untamed and rugged Barranco de los Cochinos.

The path ascends past the houses and then switches to the left along the slope above the Barranco de los Cochinos. After a quarter hour, pass a tumbledown property on the right, covered in blackberry bushes. Subsequently, enter a tributary valley only to leave it again by bearing to the left. The path now enters a sparse laurel and heath wood. About 20 min after the tumbledown property, pines also appear on the edge of the path. Almost 10 min later, the mixed forest now becomes denser and blackberry creepers hang down from the trees, the trail forks, 640 m (the path to the left descends to a *galería* at the bottom of Cochinos Gorge, 510 m, a very worthwhile excursion for botany buffs; 1 hr there and back); bear right to reach another fork some minutes later – here again to the right, ascending into the valley cleft. Some minutes later, the path merges with a forestry road (stone column *Las Moradas*, 735 m).

To the right, you can continue the hike in the direction of Las Portelas (→Alternative) however, we turn left. After 5 min, pass the ruins of a building. A few minutes later, the forestry road leads through a small valley cleft. Here, a distinctly marked path branches to the right. This merges some minutes later with an intersecting trail which we follow to the left. It leads on the level for about 5 min traversing the slope then ascends to a wide dirt road (stone column *Las Cuevitas*) which we reach after a climb of about 20 min. Take a left onto this road and head in the direction of »Las Rosas«. After a quarter hour, in a left-hand bend in the road, a forestry road with a barrier branches off to the left and a path to the right, however, continue straight ahead. A half hour later, the wood thins out – we can already see the village of Erjos before us. In the next right-hand bend (stone column *Las Rosas*) a trail branches off to the left which short-cuts the wide loop of the dirt road. After 10 min, between the first houses, reach the stone column *Pie de Erjos* and now head straight on in the direction of »El Puente«. Soon reach the church square of **Erjos**, 1000 m – behind the church, on the main road, there is a bus shelter (bus stop for lines 325 and 460).

From the church gate, continue straight on past the church square and back to the stone column *Pie de Erjos* then keep right, following the sign »Barbuzano« downward. At the last house in the row, turn left from the asphalt road onto a *camino* which zigzags down into **Barranco de Cuevas Negras**. Always remain on the main path which leads along the right side of the valley – along this stretch, the *camino* turns into a track. Now the track follows along a water conduit which has replaced the ruined watercourse. 20 min after Erjos, leave the overgrown terraces of the village behind then enter a sunny scrub wood. The wide *camino* through the forest, lined with moss-covered stones, is one of the prettiest to be found in the Teno Mountains. After 10 min, a small, almost hidden house appears to the left and a good 10 min later – now on the left side of the valley – pass a farmstead and abandoned gardens. On the other side of the slope, more houses appear. Below them, the *camino* switches to the right side of the valley once again and leads through the village **Las Cuevas Negras**, 500 m – most of the houses are in a state of disrepair, only some are inhabited by cultural drop-outs.

In the village centre, at the stone column *Barbusano*, an overgrown path branches off to the right in the direction of »Lomo Morín«, however, we head straight on, continuing our descent (there may be signs for »Susana«). The gorge now becomes more dramatic: the *camino* dips rather steeply under an overhanging and extremely furrowed rock wall; gigantic spurge plants line the edge of the trail. Before us, we can already make out Los Silos. After a good 20 min reach the floor of the *barranco* and the first houses – to the left, the mighty Barranco de los Cochinos branches off. We are greeted by what is truly a little paradise – encircled by lush gardens of orange, almond, fig, medlar and palm trees, and also later on by banana plantations. A track leads down the valley, soon crossing a bridge and switching to the right valley flank. The track now ascends slightly for a short distance and, at a house, diverges away from the stream bed. Before reaching the house, descend into the stream bed to a track on the other side (*Calle Susana*) which leads back to the main square in **Los Silos**.

Kiosk on the village square of Los Silos.

17 Cruz de Gala, 1354 m

Enchanting circuit route through laurel woods and over panoramic summits

Erjos – Cruz de Gala – Little Gala (Montaña de las Rosas) – Erjos

Location: Erjos, 1000 m.
Starting point: Restaurant »Fleitas« on the main road 1.5 km above Erjos, directly before the turn-off to San José de los Llanos (car park; bus stop for lines 325/460).
Walking times: Erjos – Cruz de Gala a good 1¼ hrs, Cruz de Gala – Little Gala 1 hr, Little Gala – Erjos 1½ hrs; total time 3¾ hrs.
Ascent: Almost 500 m.
Grade: Aside from the somewhat precipitous stretches along the cliff on Little Gala, usually an easy walk.
Refreshment: Bar/restaurants in Erjos.

This interesting circuit walk over the Gala peaks is characterised by magnificent, ever-changing panoramic views.

From the bus stop at the **Restaurant**, descend 50 m along the main road toward Erjos and then turn left onto a lane. This leads in wide bends down to a plain then, after 10 min, turns sharply to the left (not to the right!) and 30 m on merges with an intersecting track (to the left – our descent route later on). Follow this to the right. 100 m on, the track merges into a wider track that leads straight on to Erjos (on the right, an alluvial plain with a bizarre, towering crag) – turn left onto this track, passing between two ponds that are often without water. Remain on the main track passing subsequent forks (that is, a good 100 m on, pass the first branch to the right and then the second one to the left 20 m further) ascending straight along the other side of the valley to the ridge. On the ridgeline (up to this point, ½ hr total) keep left.

After 35 m, a distinct path branches off to the right which remains approximately at the same elevation leading through the laurisilva forest. After a quarter hour, keep bearing to the left on the main trail. 5 min later, the trail forks again. Here, go left to ascend through a valley cleft (after a few minutes, bear right at a fork) and to a wide forestry trail. Follow the trail to the left. After not quite 10 min it merges with another wide forestry trail. To the left, behind the *iron gate*, reach a narrow asphalt road which ascends from the Erjos Pass to Cruz de Gala.

The climb to the summit of **Cruz de Gala** – which sports a fire-watcher's tower and a radio installation – takes 15 min and offers a wonderful panoramic view :

nearly the entire Teno mountain chain lies below us (immediately to the south-west – the jaunty rock peak of the Little Gala); the volcanic world at the foot of Pico Viejo also lies before us as if served up on a platter for our enjoyment.

Back at the *iron gate* (a good 10 min) head left on the level forestry trail toward »*El Saltadero*«. After a good 10 min, the wide forestry trail hooks to the right. Here, remain on the trail continuing straight on until reaching a fork 30 m on – at this point, bear left to the next fork at the stone column *El Saltadero* (50 m) and bear left once again. The mountain trail, now ascending only moderately, leads in a quarter hour to **Degollada de la Mesa**, 1247 m, the saddle between the Cruz de Gala and Little Gala.

At the spot where the main trail leads down to the left, a path branches off diagonally to the right which leads over the ridgeline in almost a quarter hour up to the **Little Gala** (Montaña de las Rosas), 1318 m (somewhat precipitous; at the summit, some light scrambling is required). The view of Masca, the mighty Masca Gorge and Gomera is exquisite!

Back at Degollada de la Mesa, continue descending on the main trail. After 10 min, this becomes a wide forestry trail. Crossing the slope

View from Degollada de la Mesa to Cruz de Gala.

along this in not quite half an hour, reach the road leading from the Erjos Pass up to Cruz de Gala. Follow this to the right and after a quarter hour, about 200 m before the Erjos Pass, turn left at the stone column *El Pelado* onto a path (to the left – a track) that soon becomes a pleasant, wide *camino*, descending to the plain and then becomes a track (10 min) from which after 30 m another track branches off to the right, directly past a dirt mound on the right. This track brings us back to the starting point (keep right after 30 m) in a good 10 min.

18 From Buenavista to Masca via El Palmar

Varied valley walk and ridge crossing

Buenavista – El Palmar – Las Lagunetas – Las Portelas – Tabaiba Pass – Cruz de Gilda – La Vica – Masca

Starting point: Bus station in Buenavista del Norte, 119 m, or turn-off from the road to El Palmar (bus stop for lines 107/355/363/365/366).
Destination: Masca, 600 m (bus stop for line 355).
Walking times: Buenavista – El Palmar 1 hr, El Palmar – Las Portelas 1 hr, Las Portelas – La Cancela ¾ hr, La Cancela – Cruz de Gilda a good 20 min, Cruz de Gilda – Masca ½ hr; total time 3¾ hrs.
Ascent: A good 800 m, a good 300 m in descent.
Grade: Consistently pleasant walk, sometimes along roads, but mostly on pleasant *caminos* and paths.
Refreshment: Several bars and restaurants along the way (in Buenavista, El Palmar, Las Lagunetas, Las Portelas and Masca).
Alternative: Side trip from Cruz de Gilda, 780 m, to Morro de la Galera/ Roque de Masca (only for sure-footed hikers with an excellent head for heights): From the crest of the pass, a track as-

cends towards the west then ends after 5 min. Keeping left, a distinct, pleasant trail continues with a magnificent view of Masca and the Roque de Masca. The path soon switches to the right side of the ridge. Sometimes somewhat exposed, this leads over a narrow rocky ridge. Some minutes later, the ridge flattens again and the ridge leads down and slightly to the right past a small rocky plateau (¼ hr). The mountain path, with precipitous stretches, leads slightly further downhill then continues in constant up-and-down hiking along the cliff face before ascending steeply in tight zigzags. After 10 min, an unpleasantly precipitous traverse follows, then continue a steep ascent until reaching the plateau of Morro de la Galera (a total of about 1½ hrs ascent, return route 1¼ hrs).
Note: This hike can be split into two comfortable (half-)day walks (e.g. to/from Las Portelas). Each village on the walk can be accessed with bus line 355 Buenavista – Masca.

A walk could hardly be more varied: the ascent through the Palmar Valley leads us through a rural, still mostly unspoilt Tenerife. At the end, the panoramic crest of Cumbre del Carrizal awaits us. An delightful descent then leads us down to the palm groves of the beautifully-situated village of Masca.

Walk from the **bus station** up to the main road and follow this a good 100 m to the right, to reach the left turn-off of the main road to El Palmar and Masca; ascend along this for 5 min. In the first left-hand bend, turn right onto the narrow street heading straight uphill. A quarter hour later, cross the main road once again. On the other side (stone column *La Cuesta*), a cobblestone *camino* continues which subsequently crosses or touches the main road several times – little yellow metal signs indicate the route (after 10 min, you have to fol-

low the main road for 40 m). After about 20 min, at a left-hand bend in the main road, reach the stone column *Camello*. In the left-hand bend, an asphalt road branches off straight on (to the right of the main road), leading steeply past a dam wall and up through the village of **El Palmar**. In a good 20 min, where the mountain valley of El Palmar begins, once again cross the main road and continue straight on (not diagonally to the left) along the narrow asphalt road. At the stone column *El Molino*, we once again touch the main road (bus stop, bar) but go straight on and after 50 m pass the church on the right, continuing on the village street (Calle La Cruz). After 10 min, pass the stone column *Las Cuevas* (to the right, a *camino* branches off to Teno Alto, →Walk 19). Continuing straight on, pass a mighty volcanic hill, rutted by deep furrows – the lava sand surface has been sliced like pieces of cake. After a good 5 min, pass the stone column *Segovia* (to the right, a possible ascent to the Tabaiba Pass) and continue straight on 100 m to the stone column *Lomo del Medio*. Here, turn left onto a track (sign »El Callejón«). Ignore a track which soon turns off to the right – our track also bears slightly to the right and uphill after 50 m. We pass a transformer tower and past a right-hand loop of the main road (¼ hr, stone column *El Callejón*) walk straight on along the village street (Calle El Ojito) of **Las Lagunetas**.

By the church, at the village square sporting a bar, turn right and continue on the narrow street (Calle de

View from Cumbre del Carrizal into the El Palmar Valley.

La Cruz) that soon ends at a gate. To the left, a meadow path passes through terraces and merges with the main road at the school in **Las Portelas** (bus stop, stone column *Aruga*).

Cross the main road and continue uphill along the street to the right (sign »Martín Bay«). After about 100 m, in a left-hand bend, a meadow path branches off to the right then crosses a *barranco* at the bottom by bearing to the right; on the other side, immediately ascend to a road (after a few minutes, bear right at the fork). Follow the road uphill to the last left-hand bend below the main road. About 25 m after the left-hand bend in the road, a distinct, but sometimes somewhat overgrown path branches off to the right (little yellow metal signs), which reaches the main road some minutes later at the stone column *Martín Bay*. Across the road, diagonally to the left, the *camino* continues. This ascends pleasantly in wide bends and after a quarter hour reaches the ridgeline of **Cumbre del Carrizal**, 920 m (stone column *La Cancela*; you can also get here by following the main road to the right to reach the Tabaiba Pass in 15 min and, 10 m before the sharp left bend, ascend to the left on the panoramic ridgeline path, 25 min). The meteorological divide runs along the ridgeline, separating the rainy north from the sunny south-west – accordingly, the vegetation changes abruptly at the ridgeline: behind us the heath tree covered slopes of the upper Palmar Valley, before us the succulent-blanketed slopes of the Carrizales Valley.

Cross the ridgeline trail (which ascends to the left over Cumbre de Bolico to Cruz de Gala) and follow the trail that leads on the other side of the ridge towards Cruz de Gilda/Masca. This soon passes a mountain spur with a panoramic view of Los Carrizales and the *barranco* of the same name, as well as beyond to the Gilda Pass. The route continues as a beautiful mountain walk, passing a spring, to reach **Cruz de Gilda**, 780 m. To the right of the road, a track branches off and after some minutes becomes a spectacularly panoramic cliff face path (→Alternative), but we can also enjoy a marvellous view over the Masca Valley from the crest of the pass.

Now in front of the overlook platform at the pass, follow the lane that branches off to the left in the direction of Masca. Two minutes later, directly above a palm tree, a rocky path branches off to the right, descending away from the palm trees. Soon walk below a farmstead then descend in zigzags. After a quarter hour, the trail merges with the main road at the bar/restaurant »Masca« in the district of **La Vica** (bus stop).

It takes not quite 10 min to reach **Masca** along the main road, where several attractive bars and restaurants offer refreshments. Countless palm, orange, lemon and almond trees thrive in this sun-drenched valley, protected on all sides by steep rocky mountains. Is there a more beautiful place on earth?

The descent route from Cumbre del Carrizal to Masca.

19 From El Palmar to Teno Alto

Circuit walk over the Teno plateau and Cumbre de Baracán

El Palmar – Teno Alto – Tabaiba Pass – El Palmar

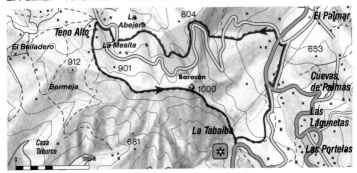

Starting point: El Palmar, 520 m, turn-off of the road to Teno Alto (bus stop for lines 355/366, parking possible on the side of the road).

Walking times: El Palmar – Teno Alto 1½ hrs, Teno Alto – Tabaiba a good 1¼ hrs, Tabaiba – El Palmar 40 min; total time 3½ hrs.

Ascent: A total of 500 m.

Grade: A usually easy walk, however from time to time somewhat overgrown and steep; possible orientation problems when cloudy or foggy.

Refreshment: Bar/restaurants in El Palmar and in Teno Alto.

Combination possible with Walks 18 (from Tabaiba Pass), 20 and 21 (from Teno Alto).

Expanses of meadowland, cultivated terraces and the occasional hamlet characterise the barren plateau of Teno Alto – walkers who experience the rough beauty of this frequently wind-blown, cloud-covered landscape when the sun is shining can consider themselves very lucky.

Begin the walk in **El Palmar** at the turn-off of the road to Teno Alto. Directly parallel (above), a *camino* (sign »Teno Alto«) leads uphill between stone walls and along a telegraph line. After almost a quarter hour cross a track (there is a nice picnic area to the right on the street) and now begin a steeper ascent. A few minutes later, cross over the road leading towards Teno Alto (stone column *Los Viñatigos*). The distinct trail (sign »El Charco«) now leads into a valley cleft and ascends steeply through sparse scrub and pine wood to a saddle on the ridgeline of the Cumbre de Baracán (20 min).

Here, meet up with the road again but do not cross over to it. Our *camino* runs parallel to the road and somewhat below it, along a conduit (after 5 min straight on at the barrier). Now, cross a valley cleft and then ascend for a short time to a rocky ridge (keep right here) and walk downhill on the other side of the ridge. The cobblestone trail first leads through cloud forest and then passes terraced cultivated fields. Now, descend along a valley cleft then bear right on the cobblestone trail at a fork. After a good quarter hour, reach the valley floor. The trail now leads along the slope again, bearing left and over a projecting rock, slightly ascending to a terrace in the slope where the *camino* widens into a track (a few houses on the right). Some minutes later, in a sharp left-hand bend in the track, the cobblestone *camino* continues straight on. Shortly after, the *camino* crosses the Teno road (stone column *San Jeronimo*) and immediately afterwards finally merges with it. Keeping left, we soon reach the church square of **Teno Alto**, 780 m, where two bars are located.

Next to the church square, turn left onto the ascending street. After a good 10 min, pass a couple of old houses and shortly after reach a fork at the stone column *Las Casitas* – here continue straight on to the nearby stone column *Las Siete*. Here, keep left, following the sign »La Tabaiba« and ascend to a small water reservoir; now, follow the path on the right which a few minutes later veers to the left away from the crest of the mountain ridge and leads along a slope through a heath tree wood. Some minutes later, the trail once again returns to the other, treeless flank of the ridge, now with a beautiful view of Los Carrizales and the west coast as well as of Gomera. The trail initially continues to the right below the ridge and some minutes later switches to the left side of the ridgeline. Later, the trail returns to the right side of the ridge and, now an hour from Teno Alto, reaches the stone column *Las Longueras*. To the left, a path branches off to **Baracán**, 1002 m (surveyor's post) however, we walk straight on, continuing in the direction of Tabaiba (sign). A good 5 min later, the *camino* changes back to the left side of the ridge, now with a pretty view of the Palmar Valley. Almost a quarter hour later, the trail once again touches the crest of the ridge (there are nice spots for a break on the other side of the ridgeline); a good 5 min later, reach the **Tabaiba Pass** and the Masca road.

20 m before the road, a distinct *camino* branches off to the left into the Palmar Valley – this descends only a short distance then leads on the level along the slope below the road and over to a house. From there, descend 30 m on the track and then to the right next to it, continue on a meadow path which soon passes another house on the left. Cross a track (5 m on – bear to the right) and soon, bearing right and walking downhill, reach a wide street; descend along this to the main road and the upper district of the village of **El Palmar** (bus stop). To the left, this road brings us back to the starting point in 10 min (if you wish to avoid the main road, you can follow the path on the other side: at an intersecting street, turn right to the village street of El Palmar and here turn left to descend to the stone column *Las Cuevas*, next to the turn-off of the road to Teno Alto).

20 Risco Trail – from Buenavista to Teno Alto

Spectacular cliff trail to the Teno Alto plateau

Buenavista – Barranco de la Torre – Teno Alto and back

Location: Buenavista del Norte, 119 m (bus stop for lines 107/355/363/365/366).

Starting point: Bridge over the Barranco del Monte on the road from Buenavista to Teno Bajo (Punta de Teno), at km 2.5 (½ hr on foot, no bus connection!). Parking possible on the side of the road.

Walking times: Bridge – Teno plateau 1¼ hrs, side trip to Roque El Toscón 35 min, plateau – Teno Alto 40 min, return route 1½ hrs; total time 4 hrs.

Ascent: About 700 m.

Grade: Sometimes very steep, often exposed cliff face ascent to the Teno plateau; when wet, this walk should not be undertaken.

Refreshment: Bar/restaurants in Buenavista and in Teno Alto.

Alternatives: Combination possible with Walk 21 (unfortunately with 1 hr of walking along a main road from the destination point of Walk 21 to the starting point of this walk and with a 10 min stretch in an unlit tunnel!). – From Teno Alto you can continue to El Palmar, Las Portelas or Masca (bus connection, →Walks 18, 19).

»Risco Trail« – what a fitting name! – the cliff face trail leads right along the steep, rock walls of the Teno Mountains plunging, sometimes sheerly, down to the plain of Buenavista – a thrill like no other, rewarded by breathtakingly beautiful downward views.

2.5 km from Buenavista, the road crosses the vast Barranco del Monte. Just on the other side of the **bridge**, before the second reservoir, a trail branches off to the left at the stone column *Mojamed* (sign »*Teno Alto*«) and, after 100 m, leads past a large water reservoir on the left. Now walk about 15 m through the stream bed of the *barranco* and then turn right toward the smaller stream bed of **Barranco de la Torre**. The hiking trail now leads about 10 min in the stream bed then leaves the *barranco* by bearing to the right and then ascends steeply along the neighbouring mountain ridge. After a total of about 25 min, a path branches off to the right at a small terrace, however, we ascend straight on (left) over steps (shortly after, bear right at the fork). Soon, a couple of metres of exposed ascent leads over steps cut into the rock. Somewhat later, traverse the slope to skirt left around a projecting rock, pass a cave then reach a

The Teno plateau – near Matoso.

steeply plunging *barranco* – this is a somewhat exposed stretch which can be very tricky when wet. The *camino* now continues up along the steep, gully-like *barranco* for about 20 min and then leaves it again towards the left, ascending to the rim of the Barranco de la Torre. After about 15 min, the trail leads to the left below a small rock wall and soon after leads to the right over a broad, reddish outcrop of rock. Some minutes later, reach the Teno plateau through a goat gate and then immediately reach the site of a circular gathering place for the ancient Guanche peoples which is enclosed by stone walls.

On the other side of the site, a narrow path continues to the right traversing the slope. After 5 min, in front of a little block peak, the path descends to the right to a beige/red-coloured, erosion-whittled landscape (now without a distinct path). About 10 min from the block peak, reach **Roque El Toscón**, a small, detached rock spur that plunges vertically down towards the coast (the last stretch requires some scrambling).

Back at the Guanche cult site follow the *camino* ascending on the other side of the cult site (little yellow signs). The sometimes stone-paved trail bears to the right past a colourful zone of tuff rock formed from volcanic ash, and then ascends, bearing right, to a wide, intersecting trail (almost 10 min) which we follow to the right, crossing over to a flat saddle (to the right – a possible ascent to Montaña de la Mulata). Past the saddle, our trail leads to the left, slightly ascending, traversing the slope and over to a flat mountain ridge; cross over the ridge then descend to a road junction (10 min, stone column *Puerto Malo*). Now cross the intersection and head straight on, ascending the washed-out gully (sign »*Teno*«; in wet weather, it is better to follow the road ascending to the right). A good 5 min later, meet up with the road again; turn left to reach **Teno Alto**, 780 m (5 min).

21 From Teno Alto to Punta de Teno

Exhilarating descent to the north-western tip of Tenerife

Teno Alto – Roque Chiñaco – Teno Bajo (– Punta de Teno)

Starting point: Village square in front of the church of Teno Alto, 780 m, on the plateau of the Teno Mountains (no bus connection, approach on foot using Walk 19).

Destination: Teno Bajo (Caserío Las Casas), 90 m. No bus connection, thus either return to Teno Alto via the same route or turn right on the road to reach Buenavista (1½ hrs, a 10 min stretch in a tunnel; fascinating, but with a risk of falling rock in stormy or rainy weather!). Alternatively, one can also return to Teno Alto from Ermita de El Draguillo at km 6.9 (after a few minutes along the road to Buenavista) then to the right on a mountain path along Barranco de la Sobaquera (about 2¾ hrs

ascent, requires sure-footedness; caution: parts of the old path are in very bad condition!).

Walking times: Teno Alto – Roque Chiñaco 1¼ hrs, Roque Chiñaco – Teno Bajo a good ½ hr; total time 1¾ hrs (return route an additional 2½ hrs; excursion to Faro de Teno an additional ½ hr one way).

Ascent: 700 m.

Grade: A pleasant descent until reaching Roque Chiñaco, afterwards, a scree-slippery descent.

Refreshment: Bar/restaurants in Teno Alto.

Combination possible with Walk 20 (see there).

The descent from Teno Alto to Punta de Teno – the north-western tip of Tenerife – is one of the most popular walks in the Teno Mountains. The route leads us through the barren fields of the Teno plateau, torn by untamed erosion gullies as well as pleasant valleys – an isolated, archaic strip of God's earth providing magnificent views of Gomera when visibility is good.

From the *plaza* in **Teno Alto**, a street leads straight on (sign »*Teno Bajo*«) which becomes a track 150 m on and then after 10 min forks on a flat ridge with a few houses – here, descend straight on. Past the stone column *Vallado*, the track continues straight on to reach the stone column *Jabuche* in a good 10 min (here, at the fork, continue descending to the right). Almost 5 min later,

View from Punta de Teno to Roque Chiñaco (left).

cross a road at the stone column *La Cueva* and descend on the old, partially cobblestone *camino* to the left of the road. This runs along a conduit on the right rim of the Barranco de las Cuevas. Some minutes later, merge with the road once more but leave it again after passing a farmstead, bearing left, along the *barranco* and parallel to conduits. Agaves, prickly pear cactus and spurge plants line the trail which then leads between the ruins of houses. The trail heads directly toward a group of houses and 10 m before the first house, turns left descending to the floor of the *barranco*. Here, meet up with the track again, following this to the left and to the other side of the *barranco*. Between terraces, the track now leads steadily downhill (after a few minutes, pass through a gate; close it again!) until it ends a quarter hour later at a land spur at **Roque Chiñaco**. The view is majestic: before us, we see the Punta de Teno with its lighthouse, behind us, the Barranco de las Cuevas.

At the end of the track, flanked by rows of stones and heading down to the left, a distinct *camino* continues. Soon pass a beautiful rock tower. After about 25 min, the trail, which at the end is unpleasantly slippery due to a great deal of scree, passes a water distributor (here, ignore a short-cut path to Punta de Teno branching off to the left along a large conduit). 5 min later, the trail forks – continue left here on the main trail which merges with the Buenavista – Punta de Teno road 5 min later (stone column *Las Casas*) next to the agricultural co-operative Luz de Teno in **Teno Bajo**.

If you wish to make an excursion to the lighthouse on Punta de Teno, follow the trail above the street to the left.

22 Guergues Path

Classic walk high above the Masca Gorge

Casas de Araza – Finca de Guergues and back

Threshing yard on the Lomo de Tablada with a view of Teide.

Locations: Masca, 600 m (bus stop for line 355), and Santiago del Teide, 930 m (bus stop for lines 325, 355, 460 and 462).
Starting point: Casas de Araza, 950 m, on the road Sanitago–Masca (bus stop for line 355). Parking at Mirador de Masca (400 m beneath the Cherfé Pass).
Walking times: Casas de Araza – rocky peak a good 1¼ hrs, rocky peak – Finca de Guergues ¾ hr, return route 2 hrs; total time 4 hrs.
Ascent: About 500 m.
Grade: A sometimes steep *camino* requiring sure-footedness and a head for heights. The path on the Guerges plateau is somewhat indistinct from disuse.
Refreshment: Bar/restaurants in Masca and in Santiago del Teide.

This walk leads over a mountain ridge separating the two most dramatic gorges of the Teno Mountains: the Barranco de Masca and the Barranco Seco. After presenting dizzying downward views into both steep gorges, the route additionally offers a splendid view from the abandoned Finca de Guergues of the cliffs near Los Gigantes – even the neighbouring island of Gomera seems only a stone's throw away. One of the most worthwhile tours on the island!

Beginning at **Mirador de Masca** descend about 200 m on the main road to reach the next hairpin bend to the right where a track to **Casas de Araza** forks off to the left. To the right of this track, a footpath forks away from the main road, descending along the mountain ridge to a gentle saddle (not quite 10 min later, ignore the left fork to Barranco del Natero). The orange-marked *camino* now leads in easy up-and-down walking then steadily ascends to the

left of the ridge (sometimes over rock; watch for cairns) – time and again, lovely views open up of the Masca Valley below. After a total of not quite half an hour, approach the ridgeline and a few minutes later, pass a small cave. Shortly after, the trail descends steeply to a small gap (a good 5 min). Passing through a gate, the *camino* resumes an ascent and subsequently leads to the left of the ridgeline, sometimes on the level and sometimes in steep up-and-down walking. Just before reaching the highest point of the walk – a prominent rocky peak crowned by a wooden post – does the *camino* switch for a short time to the right side of the ridgeline (somewhat exposed) only to return to the left side before the summit is achieved. Now reach an extended meadow plateau, the Lomo de Tablada, dropping down to the south-west, with a few houses standing at the upper end.

Before hiking down to the houses, be sure to climb the few remaining metres to the rocky peak with the wooden post, 1034 m. This offers a grand view of Barranco de Masca and most of the Teno chain, as well as of Teide and Pico Viejo. After a total of 1½ hrs reach the houses on the right-hand edge of the mountain plateau. A threshing yard shows that grain has been cultivated here in the past.

If you wish to hike down to Finca de Guergues, follow the path that leads to the left past the threshing yard. 30 m on, just below a cistern, turn right and descend along a mountain ridge, leading mostly between abandoned terraces. Beneath us, we see two solitary, dilapidated farmsteads – reach the first one after almost a quarter hour and the second – the **Finca de Guergues**, 730 m – after another quarter hour. From here, enjoy a marvellous view of the coast between Los Gigantes and Las Américas. If you still feel adventurous, you can also make an excursion without a distinct path to the south-west secondary rocky summit (½ hr one way) or to the sheer cliff's edge of the Masca Gorge (20 min one way).

23 Masca Gorge

Daring descent through the rocky labyrinth of Barranco de Masca

Masca – Barranco de Masca – Playa de Masca and back

Starting point: Centre of Masca, 600 m (bus stop for line 355), above the chapel.

Walking times: Masca – Playa de Masca 2¾ hrs, return route 2¾ hrs; total time 5½ hrs.

Descent and ascent: 600 m.

Grade: Strenuous, frequently steep walk requiring sure-footedness, a head for heights and a fair sense of direction. Never enter the gorge during unstable weather (rain or storms) or after heavy rainfall!

Refreshment: Bar/restaurants in Masca.

Note: On Playa de Masca, there is a ship's landing which, however, can only be used when the sea is calm (boat pick-up and transfer to Los Gigantes tel. 922861918, reservations required, departure from Playa de Masca daily around 1:45/3:30 p.m.; alternatively, you can join an organised walking group). Swimming is good here when the sea is calm, so remember to bring your swimming gear!

Destination for the spectacular gorge route: the boat landing at the Playa de Masca.

The chasm-like Masca Gorge, surrounded by cliff walls several hundred metres high, is an adventure in itself: passing through Masca's gardens and following a small brook, enter into an incredible labyrinth of crags and *barrancos*, the sound of the sea growing ever nearer – fantastic!

Walk down from the street to the chapel of **Masca**. Here, head left past the chapel and descend to the village district situated on a mountain ridge between the Barranco de Masca (left) and the Barranco Madre del Agua (right). Almost 10 m past a large sign and about 30 m before the bar on the mountain ridge, a walking trail branches off to the left into the Barranco de Masca. This descends directly and steeply between agave cactus and palm trees down to the stream bed and is sometimes unpleasantly slippery (always remain on the main trail which is often stepped). After about 15 min cross a little bridge (25 m on, above a pile of rubble, there is the entrance to a tunnel which leads into the Barranco Seco).

10 min later cross over again to the right bank of the stream. The idyllic path passes numerous terraces and crosses through rushes and reeds to return to the left bank. After a total of 40 min – leaving the cultivated terraces of Masca behind us – the path returns again to the right bank. The cliff walls now press in more closely. The path leads over smoothly polished rocks down to a small weir where a watercourse begins to the left; along this, we can circumvent the dam wall. Directly after, the trail continues via the stream bed, then skirts to the right around a rock blockade. We are now in a veritable rocky labyrinth – small

barrancos merge from all sides, one mountain ridge after the other encroaches with steep, sometimes overhanging, cliff walls. After a quarter hour, pass an iron gate (to the right – a wire fence) and immediately afterwards, the route is blocked by a large boulder. The path descends bearing right through a rock arch (easy scrambling).

Subsequently, the always distinct trail crosses back and forth over the stream bed. After just under an hour, another giant boulder blocks the trail – the most difficult obstacle of the walk. This can be circumvented from either side: depending on the water level, either scramble to the left down over the cascade or to the right over the boulder – to avoid the water-filled basin, climb to the left over the rock barrier.

10 m above the *barranco* floor we now see a rock arch – soon after, the trail, stone-paved along this stretch, ascends a few metres to the right and subsequently crosses the *barranco* floor to switch to the left bank. Once again, traverse the slope for a short distance then the path returns to the gravel *barranco* bed. Gradually, the sound of the sea grows nearer. The path again ascends the slope to the left then leads through terraces above the floor of the *barranco* (if you wish, you can also continue along the stream bed scrambling down through a rock arch). The cliff walls now recede and the sea appears before us. To the left, where the gorge merges into the sea, a little *finca* can be seen – to the right, a small pier leads to a mass of rock in the sea providing a boat landing.

The **Playa de Masca** is covered in gravel and smoothly polished rocks but 100 m to the left (depending on the surf and season) a strip of sand can be found; when the sea is calm – a perfect spot for a swim.

The gorge walls only recede shortly before the Playa de Masca.

24 From Tamaimo to Santiago del Teide

Through the Santiago Valley via ancient trails between villages

Tamaimo – Arguayo – Santiago del Teide – El Molledo – Tamaimo

Starting point: Main intersection in the village centre of Tamaimo, 570 m (bus stop for lines 325, 460, 462).
Walking times: Tamaimo – Arguayo 1 hr, Arguayo – Santiago del Teide a good 1¼ hrs, Santiago del Teide – Tamaimo a good 1¼ hrs; total time 3¾ hrs.
Ascent: About 450 m.
Grade: Easy walk via ancient trails connecting villages.
Refreshment: Bar/restaurants in Tamaimo, Arguayo and Santiago del Teide.
Alternative: Descent from Tamaimo to Los Gigantes (1¼ hrs).

This pleasant circuit through the Santiago Valley follows ancient trails between neighbouring villages – walkers will be enchanted by the route which passes through unspoilt natural terrain and offers outstanding views.

From the main traffic intersection in **Tamaimo**, follow the main road in the direction of Guía de Isora and after 150 m, just before the bus stop, turn left on the steeply ascending village street Calle La Rosa. After passing the last house, the street becomes a wide *camino* and crosses over a watercourse 50 m on (10 m afterward ignore a right fork). A good 10 min after the watercourse, the stone wall that has flanked the *camino* now divides at a fork – here left (then soon right) ascending along the course of the wall. 10 min later, next to the Montaña del Angel, reach the high plateau of Arguayo and then meet a wide cobblestone road that merges into an asphalt road 50 m on. Follow this to the left 50 m then in the right-hand bend leave it behind to continue straight ahead on a *camino* that branches off. This ascends gently and after a good quarter hour reaches the main street in **Arguayo**, 905 m. The route continues just on the other side of the road. 40 m on, reach the Carretera General (straight ahead – the church square), here left and in 3 min ascend to the »Museo Centro Alfarero« (traditional pottery as well as relics from the Guanche culture, Tues – Sat 10 a.m. – 1 p.m. and 4 p.m. – 7 p.m., Sun 10 a.m. – 2 p.m.).

Just after the museum, pass by a bus stop shelter (line 462) – here turn left and cross over the main road to meet the trail leading to Valle de Arriba (sign). 40 m on this gently ascending cement-paved trail reach a junction next to a water reservoir – bear left to continue. The *camino* leads in easy up-and-down walking along the western slope of the Montaña de la Hoya, offering a smashing view of the Santiago Valley and the south-west coast. 20 min later, pass

over a small rocky ridge where a view opens up of the village Las Manchas with the Montaña Bilma in the background. Now the trail descends into the broad Santiago Valley and, after 10 min, forks by a couple of pines; continue straight on the main trail. A few minutes later, the *camino* crosses a field of lava and also two dirt roads one after the other. 10 min later another *camino* merges sharply from the right; 50 m on, reach a fork and turn right to continue. Soon after, the *camino* crosses over two watercourses and then meets up with a broad trail; here turn right after 25 m to merge with the main road between Santiago del Teide and Arguayo. On the other side of the road, a distinct path continues on through the lava and leads to the right of a high stone wall. Not quite 10 min later reach a dirt road; here left, passing the cemetery (3 min; the road now asphalt) and then turn right after the playground to reach the church on the main road of **Santiago del Teide**, 930 m (not quite 10 min; bus stop for lines 325, 355, 460, 462).

Turn left on the main road and descend to the filling station (5 min) then 50 m after passing the station, fork to the right onto the broad trail leading to Los Gigantes. 10 min later, this passes above **El Molledo** and then forks – bear left (to the right, a possible ascent to Risco Blanco) and at the next fork 50 m on, bear right. The *camino* now always descends along the right rim of the Barranco de Santiago. Not quite half an hour later and shortly after a watercourse merges with the trail's edge, ignore a *camino* forking left into the *barranco*. Not quite a quarter hour later, fork off to the left onto a broad cobblestone trail which passes below a large threshing yard and changes over to the left edge of the *barranco*. Descend along the *barranco* for about 100 m until the main trail ascends slightly to the left and leads to a village street and the first houses of **Tamaimo**. Continue straight on along the street (bearing right at the first fork) to the church square and pass this to the left, following the Calle Santa Ana to the main road – 50 m to the right, return to the intersection.

25 Barranco del Infierno

Gorge walk to the highest waterfall on the island

Adeje – Barranco del Infierno and back

Starting point: Adeje town centre, 310 m (bus stop for lines 416/441/473).
Walking times: Adeje – waterfall 1½ hrs, return route 1¼ hrs; total time 2¾ hrs.
Ascent: 300 m.
Grade: An easy walk.
Refreshment: Bars and restaurants in Adeje.
Notice: The gorge is open every day from 8:30 a.m. to 5:30 p.m. The environmental protection agency has set an admission fee of 3 Euro (no charge on Sundays; children under 12 are free). Also, admission is restricted to 200 visitors per day but no more than 80 at one time in the gorge. For this reason, you should be sure to make reservations a day or two in advance (tel. 922 782885) or arrive early in the morning, otherwise be prepared to wait for hours or even to find that the gorge has been booked-out that day.

Here in »Hell's Gorge« the hiker can gather first impressions of the immense *barrancos* on the island. At the end of the beautifully-laid walking trail, a triple-tiered waterfall awaits us, plunging down from a height of 80 m and flowing year-

At first, the walking trail traverses pleasantly into the valley along a slope.

round. Unfortunately, the number of visitors is restricted due to environmental protection (see Notice).

At the church bearing left and then turning right at the Casa Fuerte, follow the steep village street leading to the upper district of the town of **Adeje**. The street ends at the bar/restaurant »Otelo« (to the left, a cement track continues) – directly behind it, at the ticket booth, a walking trail begins on the right leading into the Barranco del Infierno.

At first traverse the slope above the gorge; precipitous stretches of the trail are secured with wooden stakes. After 45 min reach the stream bed, frequently flowing with water at this point. The trail switches to the right bank and subsequently crosses the stream several times. The vegetation now becomes more lush – from time to time, blackberry and other bushes encroach the trail – the cliff walls press closer and closer to the trail, as the roar of the nearby waterfall becomes louder – a remarkable ambience! Now and again, small pools offer a refreshing dip. Then, the finale: after a few unpleasant passages, we find ourselves in front of the **waterfall**, tumbling down the mighty, sheer cliff wall in three cascades. A majestic site, shielded from the outside world; hardly a ray of sunshine can find its way into this rocky cathedral.

26 From Arona to Adeje via Ifonche

Extensive mountain route above the south-western coast

Arona – Barranco del Rey (– Roque Imoque – Roque de los Brezos) – Ifonche – Boca del Paso – Adeje

Starting point: The centre of Arona, 630 m, or the bus stop at the upper town limits on the main road in the direction of Vilaflor (bus stop for lines 112/342/416/477/480/482).
Destination: Adeje, 310 m (bus stop for lines 416/441/473).
Walking times: Arona – saddle between Roque Imoque and Roque de los Brezos 1¾ hrs, saddle – Ifonche ½ hr, Ifonche – Boca del Paso 2 hrs, Boca del Paso –

Adeje 1½ hrs; total time 5¾ hrs.
Ascent: 500 m and 800 m in descent.
Grade: Although long, a mostly easy hike.
Refreshment: Bars and restaurants in Arona, Ifonche and Adeje.
Alternative: From Adeje, possible return route to Arona (not highly recommended) – this leads through Barranco del Agua, Barranco de Fañabé and along the foot of Conde, at the end through Barranco del Rey to Arona (3¾ hrs).

The heights above Arona and Adeje present walkers with a beautiful walking paradise replete with variety and often offering magnificent downward views of the coast near Las Américas as well as into the seemingly bottomless *barrancos*. Those finding the walk from Arona to Adeje too long can begin in Ifonche (no bus connections!).

From the centre of **Arona**, ascend along the village street to the church then turn left and soon reach the main road to Vilaflor – follow this to the right (beginning with a nice stretch of pavement). Cross a *barranco* (50 m before the bridge bus stop) and then 150 m after the bridge, just past the restaurant »La Granja de Arona« turn left onto a gravel road (20 min to this point).

The gravel road soon crosses Barranco del Ancón – directly afterwards, a trail marked with white arrows branches off to the right in front of a water reservoir then ascends along a conduit and a watercourse. The trail always follows close to the edge of Barranco del Ancón, soon crosses the watercourse and another one a few minutes later then a second watercourse joins us (in the meantime the path is somewhat overgrown in places). After walking 50 min, arrive at a tumbledown *finca*. Behind the building, keep right, cross the watercourses and follow these uphill – the path is still white-marked. To the left, the beautifully-formed Roque Imoque comes into view. For a short stretch, walk between the two watercourses (do not change over to the left onto the dirt road) then the path ascends the slope, bearing right. After 10 min, once again meet up with the watercourses – here, you should cross over them to the left and have a look at the sheer drop-off into the Barranco del Rey. Now continue ascending along the watercourses and almost 10 min later, pass the cosy bar/restaurant »El Refugio« (closed Saturdays, overnight accommodation available). Remain on the dirt track for another 5 min and then turn left just past a house. At the back of the house, bearing left (not up the valley!) de-

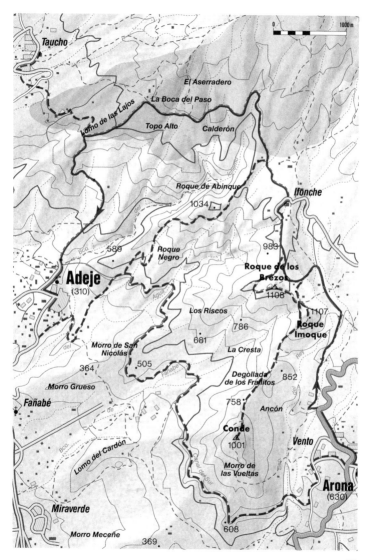

View of the caldera from Roque de los Brezos.

scend on a distinct trail along a conduit into the Barranco del Rey then on the other side and to the left of the cliff wall, ascend to the neighbouring mountain ridge. Continue ascending along the ridge to a tumbledown, solitary house. Just past this, reach a large, round threshing yard on the saddle between **Roque Imoque**, 1112 m (left, a good ¼ hr from the saddle; some scrambling required for the rocky summit) and **Roque de los Brezos**, 1116 m (right, 20 min; fabulous panoramic view). From the saddle offering us a wonderful view of Las Américas, it is also possible to descend towards Conde (almost 1 hr to the rocky foot of Conde; climbing is necessary here).

Follow the somewhat indistinct, white-marked path that traverses the eastern slope of Roque de los Brezos. After a few minutes, merge with a road that leads down to a larger farmstead – continue to the left on this road. Along the way, another path branches off to the left and leads to Roque de los Brezos, however, remain on the road which continues steadily straight on, for a short time opening a beautiful view of the coast near Playa Paraiso and Gomera, to finally reach the bar/restaurant »El Dornajo« in **Ifonche** (closed Thursdays; intersection).

Now turn left onto the street and after 100 m turn right onto a track, leaving this again 100 m later (sign) by turning left onto a pretty trail leading above a watercourse. The distinct, broad *camino* enters a sparse pine wood. After 5 min, a solitary farmstead on a mountain ridge appears ahead; the path heads towards this to the right of terraced meadows. 200 m before the farmstead, a track crosses the trail – here, it is worthwhile to take a side trip to the Infierno vista point (the hiking trail subsequently continues straight on): take a left on the track to the farmstead then descend along the ridgeline to an old threshing yard. From the mountain ridge, enjoy a beautiful view of the untamed Barranco del Infierno (even if we cannot see the waterfall) and the coast near Las Américas. By the way, a *camino* descends from the mountain ridge towards Adeje – a nice alternative (2 hrs, the trail is not maintained and sometimes overgrown).

After the side trip, continue along the marked hiking trail which leads through a sunny pine wood and uphill along a small valley cleft, leaving this some minutes later by bearing to the left. Continue a beautiful mountain walk along the slope above the chasm-like Barranco de la Fuente. After roughly 20 min, reach a fork in the trail then ascend to the right (the trail to the left leads down

Finca at the vista point by Barranco del Infierno.

to a spring and the floor of the *barranco*). Some minutes later, the path descends to the *barranco* floor and continues on the left flank to ascend back out of it again. After about 10 min, reach the crest of a mountain ridge; here, continue sharply to the right traversing the slope. In easy up-and-down walking, cross numerous, usually small valley clefts (ignore all paths forking off, therefore after a good 5 min and ½ hr later, do not bear to the right!). After 45 min, the wood thins out and we reach a flat, rocky mountain ridge on **Boca del Paso**. Straight on (bearing right) the marked trail to Taucho continues – but we turn left here along the trail descending over the flat ridge along a narrow watercourse cut into the rock. After 20 min, reach a mountain spur with a fantastic downward view of the south-west coast between Los Cristianos and Los Gigantes – here, a path branches off to the right towards Taucho, but keep left, and descend on the wide *camino* which leads in zigzags directly towards Adeje. After a good half hour, the terrain levels out and half an hour later, reach a street directly below a radio mast, taking this to the left and descending to **Adeje** – in the very first left-hand bend, a walking trail branches off to the left into Barranco del Infierno (→Walk 25) but we descend along the steep village street, bearing left at the first intersection, into the centre of town (bus stop 50 m before the church).

27 Conde, 1001 m

To the landmark of the southern island

Arona – Vento – Conde and back

Location: Arona, 630 m (bus stop for lines 112/342/477/480/482).

Starting point: Vento, 650 m, a neighbouring village of Arona. From the centre of Arona, ascend along the village street to the church then turn left onto the main road Los Cristianos–Vilaflor. Diagonally opposite to the left, the Calle Mazape forks off toward Vento (bus stop; on foot ¼ hr to house no. 78 in the Calle Vento).

Walking times: Vento – Conde 2 hrs, return route 1½ hrs; total time 3½ hrs.

Ascent: A good 400 m.

Grade: Easy to moderately difficult walk on *caminos*, some stretches on a steep path, orientation problems during periods of poor visibility.

Refreshment: Bar/restaurants in Arona.

Conde, the most distinctive mountain in the island's south, is also without a doubt one of the most beautiful panoramic summits on Tenerife. From the mountain plateau, enjoy not only a magnificent view of the south-west coast between the Reina Sofía Airport, Los Cristianos and Los Gigantes but also of the south-western caldera rim and Teide.

From the village street (Calle Vento) in **Vento**, a trail branches off in a westerly direction beside house no. 78 (sign). After 30 m bear right downhill and cross the Barranco de las Casas. On the other side of the *barranco* follow the trail marked with white arrows diagonally to the right which soon crosses the little Barranco del Ancón. The route now descends slightly, following a watercourse then drops to the right into a noticeably deeper gorge – the Barranco del Rey – a stunning

View of Conde from the harbour at Los Cristianos.

barranco typical to the southern island (if you walk a few steps down into the *barranco* floor, you will discover a remarkable cataract). Cross this gorge by walking for a total of 20 min. On the other side, the trail forks – continue here to the left on the distinct path which climbs uphill a short way and then leads along the edge of the *barranco* to the left. After a few minutes, the trail passes a dilapidated, solitary house to the right.

Beyond the house, the *camino* climbs uphill again, passing two old threshing yards one after the other and continues ascending between overgrown terraces. At the upper end of the terraced slope, the trail becomes a path again and not quite half an hour after passing the house, reaches the crest of a mountain ridge leading down from Conde. Here enjoy a marvellous downward view of the holiday resorts at Playa de las Américas and Los Cristianos.

The continued route is not quite so clear: do not proceed up the mountain ridge but instead traverse the slope before us over to the next mountain ridge lying to the west. The path is still well-marked (cairns, white arrows) – ascend the mountain ridge and after a good quarter hour reach an outcrop of rocks below a small cliff. Continue along the outcropping to the left and, bearing left, ascend along the *camino*, sometimes over rock. After a quarter hour reach the broad, slanted summit plateau of **Conde** (pay attention here to the ascent route for the return later!). Surprisingly enough, terraced fields were apparently established up here in the past but in the meantime, meadows have taken over. Now it is only 5 more min to the highest point (surveyor's post) – here are nice places to take a break.

The Anaga Massif

Rugged mountain formations and an evergreen laurisilva forest

Cruz del Carmen – the western range of the Anaga massif with Teide in the background.

STARTING POINTS FOR WALKS

Anaga mountain road

The Anaga mountain road, which runs from La Laguna to Chamorga, is one of the most picturesque and panoramic roads on the island. Secondary roads branch off from the narrow, winding road leading to interesting mountain villages previously only accessible via mule paths. The following locations are suitable for starting points for walks: Cruz del Carmen, 950 m, vista point with chapel; Centro de Visitantes del Parque rural de Anaga, farmer's market and bar/restaurant (walking trails to Las Mercedes, Chinamada, Batán and Punta del Hidalgo, among others); Mirador Pico del Inglés, 992 m, vista point on a projecting mountain spur (walking trail to Santa Cruz); bar/restaurant »Casa Carlos«, 930 m, after the turn-off of the road to Las Carboneras (walking trails to Taborno and Afur); Casas de la Cumbre, 800 m, a sprawling hamlet on the mountain road, among others – bar/restaurant »Casa Santiago« (walking trails to Santa Cruz and Afur); Casa Forestal de Taganana, 832 m, forester's house between the Casas de la Cumbre and El Bailadero (walking trails to Taganana, Afur and into the Valle Brosque); El Bailadero, 684 m, vista point with bar/restaurants (walking trails to Taganana, Almáciga and Chamorga); Chamorga, 500 m, beautifully situated village at the end of the Anaga mountain road.

From a geological standpoint, the deeply cleft Anaga massif in the north-east is the oldest part of the island. Untamed and romantic coastal cliffs, sharp ridges and chasm-like gorges characterise this mountain chain which reaches an elevation of about 1000 m on the main ridge. While the southern slopes are mostly barren and unattractive, the northern slopes are covered in a dense cloud forest – trade winds regularly bring in clouds from the Atlantic which disperse again on the other side of the main ridge. The Anaga mountain road connects the main ridge with secondary roads descending into pleasant valleys and leading to idyllic villages – a paradise for hikers and nature-lovers who, in the Mercedes Forest and the woods of the Anaga Mountains, will find rare flora including ferns up to 2-metres high as well as countless endemic plants. In addition, most villages and hamlets are connected by *caminos*, which are recently fairly well-marked.

On the coasts of the Anaga peninsula, tourist villages are scarce. Only the villages of Bajamar and Punta del Hidalgo have a tourist-based infrastructure (which is fairly modest) – both towns boast sea water swimming pools. On the other hand, along the southern coast near San Andrés, one of the island's most beautiful swimming areas has been established – Playa de las Teresitas, probably the most popular beach on the island.

Playa de las Teresitas.

91

28 From Bajamar to Tegueste

Solitary, tranquil walk through the western Anaga chain

Bajamar – Barranco de la Goleta – Moquinal (– Mesa de Tejina) – Tegueste

Starting point: Main road in Bajamar, 20 m, next to the Caja Canarias at the fork of the street leading to the sea-water swimming pool (bus stop for line 105).

Destination: Tegueste, 399 m (bus stop for lines 050–052, 058, 105).

Walking times: Bajamar – Moquinal 2¼ hrs, Moquinal – saddle at Mesa de Tejina 1¾ hrs, saddle at Mesa de Tejina – Tegueste 40 min; total time 4¾ hrs (with the excursion to Mesa de Tejina 6¼ hrs).

Ascent: 800 m and 400 m in descent (Mesa de Tejina an additional 230 m in ascent and in descent).

Grade: Mostly easy hike via paths, trails and forestry roads; sure-footedness and a fair sense of direction are essential. The ascent to Moquinal is extremely exposed to the sun.

Refreshment: Bar/restaurants in Bajamar and Tegueste.

Alternative: From Mesa de Tejina saddle to Mesa de Tejina (1½ hrs there and back, sometimes indistinct footpath and easy stretches of scrambling): From the saddle take the distinct path leading in a westerly direction, bearing left passing above a house then ascending over the ridge. Directly behind the eucalyptus tree (somewhat right of the ridge) ascend via an indistinct rocky path (watch for stepping stones and walkers' traces) along the ridge to the crest, 625 m. From here, bear somewhat to the left descending a few metres over boulders, then to the right directly over the ridge edge (easy scramble) or below the ridge to the right (somewhat overgrown) finally reaching the high plateau of the table mountain to savour a stunning view of Tegueste, Tejina, Bajamar and Punta del Hidalgo. From the left edge of the plateau, you can sometimes observe rock climbers in action.

Ascent to Mesa de Tejina.

This pleasant hike through the western Anaga chain offers no spectacular surprises, but the experience is compensated by lovely tranquil trails and scenery. Ambitious hikers, who find the tour a bit too tame, should definitely plan for the detour to Pico de Izoque and the ascent to Mesa de Tejina!

Across from Caja Canarias in the village centre of **Bajamar**, a track blocked to traffic by a chain forks away from the main street, and leads towards Mesa de Tejina bearing right. After a good 5 min, at the junction in front of the groves, bear right. 3 min later, reach a T-junction; here turn right crossing through the groves. After a good 5 min, in front of the Barranco de la Goleta, the track merges with a track that ascends from the right of the main road 150 m away. Follow this to the left, always ascending straight on. Not quite a quarter hour

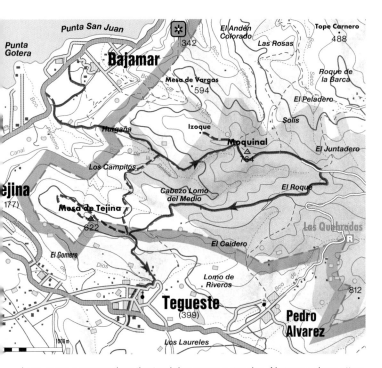

later, pass a quarry, then the track becomes a *camino*. Now pay close attention: 50 m on, a distinct path forks to the left then (25 m further on) crosses left over a watercourse. The trail now ascends to the right traversing the slope and crosses a second watercourse a few minutes later. Another 25 m leads to a fork, bear left, then shortly after, remain to the right following the main trail. This leads fairly easily through the barren, shadeless slope into the valley of the Barranco de la Goleta. Not quite ½ hr after the second watercourse, the trail forks above the ruins of a *finca*: the right fork leads through the *barranco* and over to the other side of the valley, continuing to the right over the slope then onto the Mesa de Tejina saddle (1¼ hrs, a lovely variant for the return trip) – however, bear left here to ascend easily. After 15 min, pass above a towering, solitary eucalyptus tree and begin a steeper ascent by a small valley rill. Not quite 10 min later, the now rocky and sometimes overgrown trail changes to the right flank of the valley, then back to the left flank 5 min later. After another 5 min, continue left on the main trail, then not quite 5 min later, the trail

Ascent to Moquinal – view into the Barranco de la Galeta with Teide in the background.

leads beneath and to the right of a stone wall. Passing the wall, the trail ascends for some metres, only to traverse the slope to the right, ascending along a beige rock ledge. Some minutes later, the trail hooks to the left, then soon after and 50 m before a *finca* built into a cliff, reach a fork and bear right. At a wrecked car, the trail becomes a broad, shady forestry track, that merges into the Moquinal Track not quite 10 min later. Before continuing on this to the right, bear left (straight on) over the ridge to admire a lovely view sweeping over Bejía to Chinamada. Along the track to the left, passing below the radio tower (150 m on to the left to reach the ridge), a view opens up which includes Mesa de Tejina and Teide (continuing straight ahead on this track, reach a *finca*, to meet a trail leading to the right and on to Pico de Izoque, 602 m, ½ hr., with a delightful downward view of Bajamar).

Now return to follow the Moquinal Track to the right, passing **Moquinal**, 795 m. After 15 min, a forestry road forks to the right passing through a barrier (sign »Los Dornajos«; straight on, a short excursion to the »Doctor's House« is possible: after 5 min bear left at a fork, another 5 min later, at the end of the forestry road, descend along the *camino*/steps to the ruins – near the circular terrace, the trail straight on leads to El Peladero; to the right towards Batán). The forestry road to the right descends gently at first, then not quite 10 min later (a mountain spring in a sharp right-hand bend), continues on the level through a lovely, shady heather tree and laurel forest. About 40 min after passing the spring, reach the forest **La Orilla** (»Enchanted Wood«), where the forestry road forks – here, to the right continuing through the pretty pine forest. 10 min later at a fork, continue straight on – the forest is now to the right. A few minutes later, the forestry road hooks sharply to the left and descends to a gentle valley gap, where it enters the pine forest again and then forks. A forest track forks off to the right, following the edge of the pine forest and descending along the gentle valley floor, then soon begins a slight ascent to the left along the slope. Shortly after, the track becomes a lovely trail that descends to a large threshing yard at the **Mesa de Tejina saddle** (20 min).

At the junction in front of the threshing yard, a decision must be made: a return to Bajamar can be made by turning right (2 hrs.) or the path continuing straight on ascends to Mesa de Tejina (→Alternative). However, we continue to the left descending along the *camino* to Tegueste. After 20 min the trail becomes a track (always straight on) then a street shortly afterwards. Not quite another 10 min, on the edge of Barranco de Dios, reach a fork with a street sharp to the right and a narrow street next to this to the left. Take the narrow street and 40 m on (in front of a house) turn left onto the footpath that crosses over to the other side of the *barranco* to Calle Barranco Magdalena. Now always straight on (right) to the wide village street and 150 m on, left via Calle Federico Fajardo to **Tegueste**'s parish church. Straight on, passing the city hall to the right, Calle Prebendado Pacheco leads 200 m to reach the main road and the bus stop.

The parish church of Tegueste with Mesa de Tejina in the background.

29 Mesa de Vargas, 510 m

A short excursion to the mountain ridge above Bajamar

Bajamar – Mesa de Vargas – Bajamar

Starting point: The bridge over the Barranco de Vargas on the main street in Bajamar, 20 m (bus stop for line 105).
Walking times: Ascent 1 hr; return route almost 1 hr; total time 2 hrs.
Ascent: 300 m.
Grade: Sometimes along a steep, confusing and somewhat overgrown path; sure-footedness is required.
Refreshment: Bar/restaurants in Bajamar.
Alternative: From the ridgeline of Mesa de Vargas, descent along the rocky ridge to the apartment house »Don Rafael«: After 10 min, the red-marked path bears to the right away from the ridge and descends steeply for a fair stretch over rock (Climbing Grade I). The path returns to the ridge 10 min later. Here, the route becomes increasingly difficult again

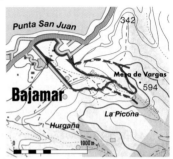

until you pass the high tension pylon to reach the apartment house (40 min; only for experienced mountain hikers with an excellent head for heights!).

The destination of this walk, a ridge sloping down from Mesa de Vargas in the direction of Bajamar, presents the seaside resorts of Bajamar and Punta del Hidalgo from a bird's-eye view.

The starting point of the walk is the road bridge spanning the Barranco de Vargas above the village centre of **Bajamar**. Continue along the main street (in the direction of Punta del Hidalgo) and after 5 min turn right onto the *Avenida Rafael G. Vernetta*. Once at the top and merging into an intersecting street, bear left and then turn right immediately afterward continuing the ascent along the *Calle Altavista*. Subsequently, walk around the Don Rafael apartment house and behind it, reach a rectangular and a circular reservoir (¼ hr up to this point).

Between the two reservoirs, a distinct path begins which leads along a conduit for a few metres then crosses to the right over an old watercourse. Ascend along this, bearing to the right, and soon reach another rectangular reservoir – the path now bears left and ascends to the conduits, continuing along these to the right. At the same time, pass between a few palm trees and after the last palm tree, reach a fork; turn right here, past a block boulder (hunting reserve sign). Just 25 m further on, a path turns off sharply to the left over a conduit then turns right (straight on leads to a small bridge – our return route later on). The path now climbs the *barranco* further up into the valley. Shortly after, the sometimes overgrown path crosses over a watercourse cut into the rock. About 20 min from the apartment house, pass a lone pine and shortly after, another pine and a huge boulder surrounded by a wall (nice place to take a break).

The path now ascends somewhat steeper and then forks 5 min later – bear left here. After a steep, 15-min ascent reach the crest of the ridge sloping down from **Mesa de Vargas** – the downwards view of Bajamar is extraordinary. If you wish, you can ascend further along the ridge to a rocky spur (5 min); from there, the view is even more encompassing. Experienced mountain hikers may choose a continued ascent over the steep, rocky terrain to Mesa de Vargas.

After an ample rest, return to the fork in front of the **little bridge** (a good ½ hr) then walk to the left to cross over the bridge. On the other side of Barranco de Vargas ascend along a path through pine woods and, after traversing the slope following along the conduits, reach a track (not quite 10 min; to the left, an excursion is possible to the head of the valley of Barranco de Vargas, 20 min to reach a stone house) then descend along this; reaching the first houses, the concrete track widens into an asphalt road and leads along Barranco de Vargas down to **Bajamar**. After 15 min, return again to the bridge on the main street (straight ahead, you can descend to the sea water swimming pools, 5 min).

View down on Bajamar from the crest of Mesa de Vargas.

30 From Punta del Hidalgo to Batán de Abajo

Classic circuit route for walkers with nerves of steel

Punta del Hidalgo – Barranco Seco canal – Bejía – Batán de Abajo – Barranco del Río canal – Punta del Hidalgo

Starting point: Church on the main road in the centre of Punta del Hidalgo, 70 m (bus stop for line 105).

Destination: End of the main street in Punta del Hidalgo at the traffic circle with the monument (last bus stop for line 105). From there, 10 min along the main street back to the church.

Walking times: Punta del Hidalgo – Bejía 2 hrs, Bejía – Batán de Abajo ¾ hr, Batán de Abajo – Punta del Hidalgo 1¾ hrs; total time 4½ hrs.

Ascent: About 600 m.

Grade: Strenuous hike requiring absolute

sure-footedness and a head for heights, especially during the descent from Batán de Abajo (steep cliff path). This precipitous route leads for a long time through a narrow watercourse, so it is crucial to restrict yourself to a small daypack; for the 50-metre stretch through a tunnel, be sure to bring a torch along.

Refreshment: Bar/restaurants in Punta del Hidalgo and in Batán de Abajo.

Combination possible with Walk 32.

Important notice: This walk should only be undertaken in dry weather and certainly not after rainfall.

Hardly a circuit walk on the island has so much to offer: untamed gorges, watercourses ingeniously cut into the rock, the tranquil mountain valley of Bejía, the secluded village of Batán de Abajo and, last but not least, the vertiginous cliff face footpath into the Barranco del Río – a unique experience for the adventurous walker!

From the church in **Punta del Hidalgo** walk a few steps along the main street then turn right onto the steep village street *Camino El Callejón*. After a quarter hour, leave the last houses of the village behind. Looking back, we can now enjoy a beautiful view of Punta del Hidalgo; below to the left, we can see the Barranco Seco. 15 min later, at the last cultivated terraces, the asphalt road becomes a gravel road. Pass two power pylons then the track descends slightly and becomes a path. Diagonally across from us, we can already see the watercourse that will dictate the further route: first cross the little tributary valley and then pass above a small water reservoir. Directly above the reservoir, a path branches off to the left from the ascending main trail. The path ascends slightly following a gully and traversing the slope, then crosses another tributary valley. After passing the edge of the next terrain, reach the **watercourse**, at this point still intact (a total of 1 hr walking from the start). This leads at a giddy height directly along the steep rock cliff above the Barranco Seco into the valley – short tunnels, galleries and the sometimes overhanging rock wall combine to create a quite exciting and varied route along, as well as in, the watercourse. After about 25 min, cross two little bridges and a short time later reach the longest tunnel in this watercourse walk (not quite 50 m; be careful not to bump your head on the ceiling). 20 m after the tunnel, circumvent an overgrown stretch by bearing to the left on a distinct path then follow the watercourse once again to its terminus at a little dam wall at the floor of the Barranco Seco – here the gorge is closed by a small cliff wall over which a waterfall cascades after periods of rain.

Now follow the path that initially runs along a water conduit and then steeply ascends to the right of the cliff over rock steps. A few houses belonging to the sprawling settlement of **Bejía** appear – on the right, at the first house, the trail merges into a road that steadily continues the climb up.

The ascent along the road offers us an unforgettable impression of one of the most idyllic mountain valleys

Walking the watercourse above the Barranco Seco.

One of Tenerife's most idyllic spots – the hamlet of Bejía.

on the island: lush gardens, quaint farmsteads, cave dwellings and ochre-coloured cliffs characterise this picturesque landscape. On the way, a walking trail merges from the right, coming from the Las Rosas ridge. After 20 min, on the ridgeline of the mountain promontory to the left (high tension pylon; sign »Bejía«) enjoy a wonderful downwards view into the untamed gorge of the upper Barranco del Río, through which our descent will lead – on the other side of the *barranco*, we can make out the cave settlement of Chinamada. Walk a good 150 m more along the road up to a distinct path which branches off to the left in front of a house (sign »Batán«). This ascends on the left side of the ridge for a short distance and then, while opening dizzying downward views, leads over to a small saddle with a high tension pylon. On the other side of the saddle, descend on steep steps cut into the rock then bear left when merging with an intersecting trail (small picnic area with a dripstone cave) down to the nearby mountain village of **Batán de Abajo**, 470 m (bus stop for line 074 at the end of the asphalt street).

In the village, directly before (above) the bar »Emiliano« (by bearing right, you would reach the end of the street with the bus stop) the signposted descent route to Punta del Hidalgo branches off to the left. This leads downward for a short distance to the cultivated terraces of the village and after 200 m, forks; here ascend to the left, past a bench cut into the rock and traverse a gentle saddle enjoying a beautiful view of Chinamada (10 min). On the other side of the saddle, bear sharply to the left and descend, always following the main trail, past terraced vineyards. After 10 min, leave the last terrace behind. The descent now appears more alpine in nature – leading over rocks and down a steep ridge with staggering downward views into a gorge to the right. This nail-biting stretch lasts for only 10 min, marking the end of the most unpleasant part of the route – but we should not get over-confident just yet because the further descent along the ridgeline of the mountain ridge is quite tricky. After 20 min, reach the floor of Barranco del Río to continue a descent to the left. Directly below a huge boulder, with a tumbledown stone house behind it, a watercourse begins at a little dam wall, however, it is very overgrown here and, due to an overhanging rock 50 m on, almost impossible to circumvent. Therefore, first follow the path that descends along the right flank of the stream bed and after about 200 m – in front of a ledge jutting in from the left – ascend along the path over a water pipe and up steps to the **watercourse** to continue the walk (if water is flowing in the watercourse, descend through the *barranco*). Although the watercourse boasts no galleries or tunnels, it does offer attractive views of the wild rocky terrain of Barranco del Río. After about half an hour of walking along the watercourse, Punta del Hidalgo appears before us. 15 min later, pass above a round reservoir, across from which we see the walking trail to Chinamada that begins below the prominent Roque Dos Hermanos. The watercourse turns a corner and Punta del Hidalgo comes again into view. Immediately afterward, leave the watercourse by turning right onto a descending track. Soon cross a bridge, then at a barrier bear left on a track up to the traffic circle at the end of the main street in **Punta del Hidalgo** (follow this for 10 min to return to the church in the centre of town).

The sprawling mountain village Batán de Abajo; Chinamada perches on the far ridge in the background.

31 From Punta del Hidalgo to Las Carboneras via Chinamada

Grand ascent through a bizarre craggy terrain to some cave dwellings

Punta del Hidalgo – Chinamada – Las Escaleras – Las Carboneras

Starting point: Traffic circle at the end of the main street in Punta del Hidalgo, 70 m (last bus stop for line 105).
Destination: Las Carboneras, 620 m (bus stop for line 075).
Walking times: Punta del Hidalgo – Chinamada 2 hrs, Chinamada – Las Escaleras a good 1 hr, Las Escaleras – Las Carboneras 20 min; total time 3½ hrs (return route from Las Carboneras to Punta del Hidalgo an additional 2 hrs).
Ascent: 700 m and a good 100 m in descent.
Grade: A somewhat strenuous walk on a

camino requiring sure-footedness
Refreshment: Bar/restaurants in Punta del Hidalgo, Chinamada and Las Carboneras.
Alternative: From Las Escaleras to Cruz del Carmen (¾ hr; bus stop for lines 073, 075-077): Ascend straight on up to the road; follow this to the right and after 15 min turn right on the level dirt road. After 10 min reach a wide *camino* on the left which ascends to Cruz del Carmen ending at the bar/restaurant of the same name on the Anaga mountain road.
Combination possible with Walks 32 and 33.

The walk from Punta del Hidalgo to the cave dwellings of Chinamada is one of the most popular routes on Tenerife – not without reason, as we will see!

From the traffic circle at the end of the main street in **Punta del Hidalgo**, head along the asphalt road leading down to the left from which a concrete-paved track soon branches off to the right (sign »*Chinamada*«). Enjoying a view of Roque Dos Hermanos, soon pass through a barrier and then pass a somewhat tumbledown building to reach the floor of Barranco del Río.

At the stream bed, bear 50 m to the right and up (left to the coarse-gravel beach Playa de los Troches) until a wide, fortified *camino* ascends to the left over a foot-bridge. The *camino* now ascends steadily and up the valley, with a beautiful view of Barranco del Río. After a quarter-hour ascent, pass a small cave. The trail now runs between beautifully cleft and hollowed-out cliff walls, and a good 5 min later, leads past a mighty ledge separated in the middle by a black lava wall. Now reach a small valley cleft in which the *camino* ascends in zigzags until bearing to the right again at a corner. After a total of 1¼ hrs, reach a fantastic spot to take a break on the ridgeline with dizzying views of the ocean. Now the path winds once again towards the slope on the *barranco* side. After 45 min ascent, sometimes steep, sometimes easy, reach the first cultivated terraces of **Chinamada**, 590 m; the cave dwellings will also soon be in view.

At the church (water source; to the left – the bar/restaurant »La Cueva«, closed Mon. and Tues.; a clearly signposted detour to one of the most spectacular vista points on the island – Mirador Aguaide; a good 10 min) meet up with a street. After 5 min, on the crest of the ridge, a smaller street branches off, continuing straight on then immediately ends at a farmstead (the first street continues toward Las Carboneras, a good ½ hr). A pretty *camino* continues, changing sides of the ridgeline three times to finally continue on the right side along the slope. Ferns, horn clover, laurel and heath tree wood surround the beautiful mountain path, passing high above the widely branching network of gorges making up the Barranco del Tomadero. Passing a few houses hidden in the wood, reach an abandoned farmstead on a mountain saddle after a good half hour. The path leads around the house and ultimately ascends steeply onto a saddle with a high tension pylon (**Las Escaleras**). Here, the path forks – straight ahead leads to Cruz del Carmen (→Alternative) but we descend sharply to the left to the other side of the ridgeline towards Las Carboneras. In a quarter hour, over steps at the end, reach a road (take a left here) which brings us in 5 min to the village square of **Las Carboneras**.

32 From Cruz del Carmen to Chinamada

Extensive circuit route through one of the loveliest valleys in the Anaga chain

Cruz del Carmen – Chinamada – Batán de Abajo – Cruz del Carmen

Starting point: Cruz del Carmen, 950 m, on the Anaga mountain road (bus stop for lines 073, 075-077).
Walking times: Cruz del Carmen – Chinamada a good 1½ hrs, Chinamada – Batán de Abajo 1¾ hrs, Batán de Abajo – Cruz del Carmen 2 hrs; total time 5½ hrs.
Ascent: 700 m.
Grade: Mostly a pleasant and easy hike via good trails; some stretches on the narrow *camino* from Chinamada to Batán, however, require sure-footedness and a good head for heights (somewhat precipitous steps cut into the rock).
Refreshment: Bar/restaurants at Cruz del Carmen, in Chinamada and Batán de Abajo.
Combination possible with Walks 30, 31 and 33.

This lengthy circuit route through Barranco del Río is still largely unknown and an absolute treat for Anaga fans – and also offers numerous combination possibilities.

A broad *camino* begins to the right of the bar/restaurant **Cruz del Carmen**; always bearing to the right, descend along this through the cloud forest. After 20 min, this merges with a dirt forestry road (Pista de las Hiedras) – follow this to the right in not quite 10 min to the road leading to Las Carboneras. Here, descend to the left and after 15 min (soon after passing a couple of houses) turn left onto the *camino* towards Chinamada. After 5 min at a fork, continue straight on (left) past the high tension pylon (**Las Escaleras**, to the right a descent possible to Las Carboneras →Walk 31, the sharp left leads to Batán). Subsequently, always remain on the main trail. This leads along a heavenly high route traversing the slope (after a good 10 min passing a house) and after 45 min merges into a road (5 min to the left on the road reach the church square of **Chinamada**, 590 m, and the bar/restaurant »La Cueva«, closed Mon. and Tues.).

Pay close attention here: directly at the merge, our route forks to the left towards Batán; the *camino* leads fairly pleasantly at first, traversing the slope, but later descends sometimes quite steeply. After 25 min, reach the most difficult stretch of the entire walk: the trail descends over a steep, somewhat exposed rock with steps that have been cut in only foot lengths (extremely unpleasant when wet). Immediately after, the *camino* crosses Barranco del Tomadero (through the stream bed, 10 m to the right) and ascends steeply for

a short stretch on the other side; after 5 min continue to the right along a cliff face to reach a breach in the rock on a mountain ridge. For the next 20 min, the *camino* leads in easy up-and-down walking along the slope, then descends to Barranco del Río, 300 m. Arriving at the valley floor, follow the distinct trail that ascends along the left flank of the valley. After a good 5 min, the trail crosses over to the right flank (just after passing a trail forking left towards Las Escaleras) then forks 50 m on. Here left, continuing along the stream bed (to the right, another possible ascent to Batán). Shortly afterward, the trail leads a good 10 m over a rocky ledge in the stream bed, then returns to the left flank, only a few minutes later to ascend through terraced fields, passing to the right of a couple of houses (a trail forks to the left towards Lomo de los Dragos; on the right valley flank – Cueva del Lino). Past the houses, cross over a bridge spanning Barranco del Río and ascend in 20 min – always following the lantern-lined way through the idyllic village – to the *plaza* of **Batán de Abajo**, 470 m.

In front of the bar/restaurant »Emiliano« cross over left to the road (bus stop for line 074) and continue the ascent along this. Not quite 10 min later, a dirt road forks to the left and 15 min later, after passing through a tunnel for about 150 m, ends at a turnabout. Here, a lantern-lined trail continues, descending to Barranco del Río. Turn left crossing the bridge and then continue to the right into the valley (in front of the first house, again to the right). Soon after, reach the stream bed and bear left along this. The *camino* ascends pleasantly along the right flank and up the valley, clearly leaving the valley floor below. After 15 min, pass numerous eucalyptus trees, then a few minutes later, meet up with the Pista de los Dragos. 50 m on to the right, the old stone-paved trail turns sharply left to continue. This ascends in zigzags on a wooded ridge and, after a half hour crosses over the Pista de las Hiedras. 15 min later, the wide *camino* merges into a forestry road (100 m on the right – the Casa Forestal); take this to the left, then always straight on, to return in 20 min to **Cruz del Carmen**.

33 Roque de Taborno

Exposed circuit route around the »Tenerife Matterhorn«

Las Carboneras – Taborno – Roque de Taborno – Taborno

Starting point: Las Carboneras, 620 m (bus stop for line 075).
Destination: Taborno, 620 m (bus stop for line 075).
Walking times: Las Carboneras – Taborno 1 hr, circuit around Roque de Taborno 1¼ hrs; total time 2¼ hrs.
Ascent: About 200 m.
Grade: Circling around the Roque de Taborno requires sure-footedness and a head for heights.
Refreshment: Bar/restaurants in Las Carboneras and Taborno.
Alternatives: From Taborno to Casa Carlos (1 hr): A *camino* forks off to the left at the bus shelter at the village limits; ascend 10 min along the ridgeline then traverse to the right through a laurel wood. After 5 min bear right at the fork following telegraph poles to ascend to the Anaga mountain road and the bar/restaurant »Casa Carlos«, 880 m (bus stop for line

077). Turn right onto the road ½ hr (right at the intersection) to reach Ermita Cruz del Carmen (bus stop for lines 073, 075, 077; bar/restaurant).

Combination possible with Walks 31, 32 and 34.

At 706 m, the Roque de Taborno (also known as the »Tenerife Matterhorn«) is by no means one of the highest but surely one of the most celebrated peaks on the island. From up close, the summit does not have the same appeal as it does from afar but the bird's-eye views of the coast that open up during the often somewhat precipitous walk around the foot of this towering peak more than compensate for the anti-climax.

From the bus stop in **Las Carboneras**, retrace about 100 m on the main road and, across from the bar/restaurant »Valentin«, turn left onto a lane from which, after 50 m in a left-hand bend, the old connecting path to Taborno forks off. This descends for a short stretch between terraces and then traverses the slope without much change in elevation. After 5 min, pass a power pylon and then a second one shortly after. Now the *camino* descends through terraces and scrub wood to Barranco de Taborno. After a final, small valley notch (a good ¼ hr) the trail ascends steeply to a road leading to **Taborno**; here turn left and, in 10 min, reach the village perched on a mountain ridge – the views are splendid.

Continue the walk by passing to the right of the chapel. 50 m on, bear right and pass numerous cave dwellings. A few minutes later, a stepped trail forks

The Roque de Taborno, one of the most unique mountains of the Anaga range.

off to the left – here continue straight on. The cemented trail descends to a saddle and then continues on the right side of the ridge. 50 m on, ignore a right fork – a *camino* leading to Playa de Tamadite – then pass a final house and reach the ridgeline by passing through a gate for goats. The Taborno peak now towers before us and the Playa de Tamadite can be seen below to the right. Shortly after, a footpath forks to the right but we remain on the ridge (actually a little to the left of it) and then, below a stone hut with a roof of corrugated iron, reach the foot of **Roque de Taborno**.

Bearing left, an almost level green-marked footpath continues a traverse of the slope, then another path forks to the left 5 min later – but here continue straight on. A little later, along our overgrown and from time to time unpleasantly precarious path, pass a rock overhang/shelter. Soon after, the path ascends steeply along a ridge towards the summit and, just below the base of the rocky peak, meets an intersecting path. Here, turn left and in a few minutes reach an extended rocky plateau, 588 m (almost ½ hr from the stone hut) with a stupendous view of the northern coast: to the east, the view sweeps over Playa de Tamadite and Playa de San Roque to Roques de Anaga; to the west, the Punta del Hidalgo juts out. Returning to the last stretch of mountain ridge, continue the ascent on the path until reaching the base of the peak. Here, the green-marked path bears to the left towards the slope and, continuing straight ahead, passes a cave serving as a goat stall. After another 15 min, back at the stone hut with the corrugated iron roof, the path merges again with our approach route, leading us back to the bus stop in **Taborno**.

34 From Taborno to Playa de Tamadite

Stimulating descent to the secluded Tamadite Beach

Taborno – Afur – Playa de Tamadite – Afur

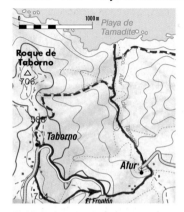

Starting point: Church square in Taborno, 620 m (bus stop for line 075).

Destination: Afur, 230 m (bus stop for line 076).

Walking times: Taborno – Afur 1¼ hrs, Afur – Playa de Tamadite a good 1 hr, return route to Afur 1½ hrs; total time 4 hrs.

Ascent: 300 m and about 700 m in descent.

Grade: An easy walk until reaching Afur. From here to Playa de Tamadite, sure-footedness and a head for heights are required.

Refreshment: Bar/restaurants in Taborno and Afur.

Alternatives: From Playa de Tamadite to Taganana (a good 1½ hrs; spectacular, exposed coastal path, several ascents and descents). From Afur to Taganana (→Walk 32, 1¾ hrs). From Afur via Inchirés to Casa Forestal de Taganana (1¾ hrs) or via Roque Negro to Casas de la Cumbre (1¼ hrs on a road, then left on a *camino* following power lines in ½ hr to the mountain road; bus stop for lines 076, 077).

From **Playa de Tamadite back to Taborno** (1¾ hrs; only for sure-footed hikers with an excellent head for heights): The path branches off from the trail 15 min before Playa de Tamadite (see below) ascending steeply (somewhat overgrown). At the fork next to a terrace, go left uphill; soon after, on the intersecting trail, continue along the stone wall. The path now traverses a small valley cleft with a few houses and then forks again; here, go left ascending through the valley cleft. Repeat the same manoeuvre at the next fork 50 m on. The path now continues steadily on the right side of the valley. Only after 10 min, shortly before a giant boulder in the stream bed, does the path lead into the stream bed for about 10 m. Subsequently, on the left side of the valley climb very steeply over stepping stones, past terraces and then left through a field up to an overhanging cliff wall; the main trail skirts this to the right and then, before the next cave, to the left over a somewhat precarious stretch of rock steps. Shortly thereafter, climb over a small rock barrier into the tributary valley to the left. Here, along the rim of the little gorge, continue further up the valley. After 10 min the path runs directly along the stream bed for almost 100 m and then ascends to the right over rock steps. Soon pass terraces on the right to reach a fork after a short, level stretch – here, turn right onto the main trail uphill. This soon bears to the left again to the valley floor and then ascends to a fork (not quite 5 min). Here, straight on (left) onto the left flank of the valley. The path at first traverses the slope then heads right through a sparse scrub wood ascending to a mountain ridge; ascend along this to the ridgeline and the first houses. Here, reach a wide intersecting trail (→Walk 30). Turn left onto the trail and return in 10 min to the church square in Taborno.

The Tamadite Gorge provides Nature-lovers with a sneak preview of the more famous Masca Gorge: here too, the walk follows along a small brook. The gorge is not quite as spectacular as the one at Masca but it is rugged enough. At the beach, a small *finca*, with buoy decorations that enhance a pleasant atmosphere, awaits us. If you prefer to avoid the descent from Taborno – one of the most impressive scenic routes on the island! – you can start the walk in Afur.

There are two possibilities for the first stage of the walk: the walker can start at the church square in **Taborno**, following the street descending on the right and ending in El Frontón (when wet, the better choice; not quite ½ hr). The prettier route starts at the turn-round at the village limits (bus stop) ascending the stone-paved camino then, after 10 m, turning left onto a lovely path that traverses the slope mostly on the level and above some terraces. After a good 5 min, bear right at the fork, then again to the right not quite 10 min later. Some minutes after this (shortly past a gate) reach a ridgeline. Here descend to the left along a wide *camino* to reach the end of a street in the settlement of **El Frontón** (¼ hr). The *camino* continues descending along the ridge and, 40 m on, before reaching a house, the *camino* changes to the right side of the ridge (water source) and descends again, soon passing more houses. After a good 20 min, at a gentle saddle, a trail merges from the right. Shortly after, the now cement-paved *camino* passes a small, picturesque cluster of houses built into the crags, skirting to the right past the houses and finally descends (ignore the left fork onto a dirt road) in steep bends to Barranco de Tamadite; through the *barranco*, finally reach **Afur**'s *plaza*.

To the right and past the little church, a cement trail continues the descent and becomes a footpath after passing the last house. The path always bears right traversing the slope, crossing over a dirt road and a track after a total of 5 min. Shortly after, pass a massive black boulder and now continue above the valley floor, traversing in a swing to the left along the slope. 5 min later, immediately after a low cliff wall, the trail forks in front of a gigantic beige-coloured boulder – here continue sharply to the right (sign). At first, a short ascent, then continue over precipitous rock steps, sometime scree-covered, leading over to the next valley gap. From here, descend steeply over steps to the brook (a good 10 min). The green-marked path now switches to the left bank and ascends past a cascade. After passing another valley rim, reach yet another and here relish a view of Playa de Tamadite before us (¼ hr). Our route now leads below terraces (above us – a little house) down to the next small intersecting valley rim (small rocky plateau; 5 min). Here, two paths branch off to the left (the ascending path to the left leads to Taborno, →Alternative) – stay on the main trail that descends to the right almost to the stream bed. Past terraces, ascend slightly again before the path finally enters the stream bed. Shortly before reaching the beach, the path forks – to the right, along the slope, a path branches off to Taganana but we change over to the left bank and pass a stone hut to reach **Playa de Tamadite**.

35 Vueltas de Taganana – from the Casa Forestal to Playa de San Roque

Classic route through a laurel wood

Casa Forestal de Taganana – Taganana – Playa de San Roque

Starting point: Casa Forestal de Taganana, 832 m, on the Anaga mountain road (bus stop for line 077).
Destination: Taganana, 200 m, or Almáciga, 60 m (bus stops for line 246).
Walking times: Forestry house – Taganana 1½ hrs, Taganana – Almáciga ¾ hr; total time 2¼ hrs (return route an additional 2½ hrs).
Descent: A good 800 m.
Grade: Easy walk on a pleasant *camino* which is slippery when wet.
Refreshment: Bars and restaurants in Taganana and Playa de San Roque.
Alternatives: From Taganana to Afur

(1¾ hrs): On the *camino* ¼ hr back in the direction of the Casa Forestal then to the right towards Afur. The trail soon crosses a dirt road (after 100 m to the left) and ascends along a power line. After ¾ hr reach a mountain pass – here turn sharply to the right over to the other side of the ridgeline via the descending trail. After ¼ hr, at a farmstead, descend on a steep, cement-paved track further to the valley road (almost ¼ hr; bus stop); here turn right and after ¼ hr reach Afur (last bus stop for line 076).
Combination possible with Walks 36 and 39.

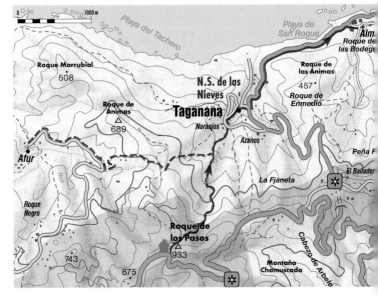

One of the showpieces of Tenerife – the vineyard village of Taganana.

This walking trail, called »Vueltas de Taganana«, leads through one of the best preserved laurisilva forests on the island: gigantic fern fronds up to two metres high and the dense, lichen-covered laurel wood flank the defile-like *camino* descending in sweeping bends to Tagana.

Left of the **forestry house**, follow the trail branching off to the right (sign »*Taganana*«). This ascends to a walled-up cave (go straight on here) and then leads on the level through a laurel wood. After about 10 min, continue straight on, the wide path now zigzagging down in countless bends. After a total of 50 min, the mountain wood thins out. Subsequently, cross Barranco de la Iglesia and continue downhill along the left edge of the *barranco* and after a quarter hour reach a turn-off – to the left, the *camino* heads towards Afur but our route leads straight on to Taganana (sign). 10 min later reach the village limits. Passing a small palm grove, reach an asphalt road and follow this to the right. After a few minutes, a set of stairs leads to the left passing one of the largest dragon trees on the island and down to the invitingly pretty village square of **Taganana** with a parish church.

At the end of the square, continue the descent passing to the left of a chapel and a short time later reach a bend in the main road. A footpath below the houses short-cuts the wide bend in the road (at the bottom to the right over the bridge) then we need only to follow the main road which brings us in 25 min to Playa de San Roque and the hamlet of **Roque de las Bodegas**. Several restaurants (serving fish specialities) and a small lava beach await the walker here. If you continue to follow the road, a few minutes later (right at the intersection) you will reach the village of **Almáciga**.

36 From El Bailadero to Almáciga

Descent from the Anaga main ridge to Playa de San Roque

El Bailadero – Taganana Road – Almáciga – Playa de San Roque

Starting point: El Bailadero, 684 m, on the Anaga mountain road (bus stop for lines 077, 247; also, bus stop »El Bailadero« for line 246 at the southern entrance to the road tunnel through the Anaga main ridge: across from the bus stop, bearing right after 5 min, ascend to the hamlet of El Bailadero with the bar/restaurant »El Balcón de Anaga«).
Destination: Almáciga, 60 m (bus stop for line 246).
Walking time: Almost 1½ hrs (return route an additional 1¾ hrs).
Descent: 700 m.
Grade: Short and easy walk on a some-times pleasant, sometimes overgrown and bumpy *camino*.
Refreshment: Bars and restaurants in El Bailadero and Playa de San Roque.
Combination possible with Walks 35 and 39. Ideal as a follow-up to Walk 37.

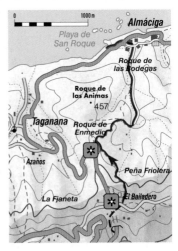

El Bailadero, ignoring the unsightly houses of the hamlet, is a wonderful eyrie: from the ridgeline, gaze down with a bird's-eye view of the coast between Taganana and Almáciga. Frequently, however, trade wind clouds sweep over the ridge and only a shadowy, fog-enveloped landscape can be seen.

Directly after the concrete structure of the bar/restaurant »El Balcón de Anaga« in **El Bailadero**, a cobble-stone trail branches off to the left entering a dense heath tree and laurel wood. This descends in zigzags along the slope of a mountain ridge and occasionally opens a beautiful downwards view of Taganana. After

The attractive Playa de San Roque is the destination of the walk.

10 min, the *camino* crosses the ridgeline of the mountain ridge (an excellent panorama of Taganana and Almáciga) above the rock tower Peña Fiolera but returns to the left side of the ridgeline 10 min later after skirting Peña Fiolera. A good 5 min later reach the **main road** to Taganana and descend along this for 200 m, leaving it again at a sharp left-hand bend directly in front of the rock tower on the right-hand side of the road, taking the path branching off to the right. The trail forks after just a few minutes – bear right, descending over the mountain ridge. To the left, we see the striking Roques de Enmedio and de las Ánimas. After 20 min, the path forks twice in a row; at both forks continue straight along the main path which keeps to the right downhill. The *camino* crosses a valley after 5 min and directly after the house descends left in 5 min to the valley floor to reach a track ending here. The track brings us to **Almáciga** in 20 min and then merges with an asphalt street.

Continue on this street, keeping left and heading downhill, and continue on the coastal road to the left to the hamlet of **Roque de las Bodegas** on the Playa de San Roque. Several restaurants serving fish and a small, partly sandy, volcanic beach await us. The end of the bay is closed by the rocky peninsula of Las Bajas stretching far into the ocean (underwater cave) and can be walked via a path protected by guard rails.

37 From Chamorga to El Bailadero

Beautiful ridge walk through an enchanting laurisilva forest

Chamorga – Cabezo del Tejo – Chinobre – Parque Forestal – El Bailadero

A stretch of the Ridgeline Trail.

Starting point: Chamorga, 500 m, at the end of the Anaga mountain road (bus stop for line 247).

Destination: El Bailadero, 684 m, on the Anaga mountain road (bus stop for lines 077, 247; also, bus stop »El Bailadero« for line 246 at the southern entrance to the road tunnel through the Anaga main ridge, 10 min: directly behind the Casa Domingo, on a distinct path, after a few minutes bearing left, downhill).

Walking times: Chamorga – Cabezo del Tejo ¾ hr, Cabezo del Tejo – Chinobre ¾ hr, Chinobre – El Bailadero 1¼ hrs; total time 2¾ hrs (return route 2½ hrs).

Ascent: A total of about 600 m and 300 m in descent.

Grade: Easy walk on a consistently pleasant *camino* which, however, is slippery when wet.

Refreshment: A bar in Charmorga, bar/restaurants in El Bailadero.

Combination possible with Walks 36 and 38–40.

The mountain route from Chamorga to El Bailadero is one of the most impressive walks, not only in the Anaga Mountains, but of the entire island: hardly anywhere on Tenerife will you find a more beautiful laurisilva forest or a vista point in the Anaga Mountains to compare to the one at Cabezo del Tejo – and when wisps of fog sweep over the crest, the walker will be inescapably whisked away into a realm of fairy tales and demons.

From the car park at the end of the main road, directly in front of the church of **Chamorga**, follow the cement track ascending to the left (*Camino La Rosalta*) but leave this by continuing straight on the *camino* following a brook. After a good 10 min, bear right at a fork. The *camino* crosses the brook and leads along the right side of the valley, continuing an ascent to a trail junction on the ridgeline of the Anaga main ridge (½ hr from Chamorga). Turn left to ascend along a steep path, at the end over steps, and in a good 10 min reach the overlook **Cabezo del Tejo**, 750 m. Enjoy a downwards view of the coast far below between El Draguillo and Almáciga.

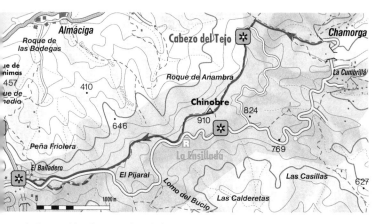

A dirt road leads up to the platform – walk along it for a few metres to the left then continue the ascent on the *camino* that branches off (sign »Chinobre«). The steeply stepped stretch lasts for only 5 min then the path continues in gentle up-and-down walking. Soon pass to the left of the mighty **Roque de Anambra**, a godlike finger of rock jutting up from the ridge and a sacred object for the Guanche aborigines. A good 10 min later, a large block boulder on the way provides a view of Anambra. The higher we climb, the more impressive the laurisilva forest becomes: trees and shrubs are covered in thick moss and the fern fronds tower higher and higher. After 40 min (from Cabezo del Tejo) a trail merges on the left from the Anaga mountain road (sign »Chamuscada«) – here continue straight on (sign »El Bailadero«). About 100 m further, a trail branches off to the right, climbing to the summit of **Chinobre**, 910 m – the 3-min ascent is rewarded by a marvellous view to the west.

After the detour, return to the mountain ridge trail then descend to the right in a good 10 minutes, at last along a wide track, past tent sites (picnic area **Parque Forestal La Ensillada**) to reach the Anaga mountain road. Follow this to the right for a good 5 min until another distinct trail branches off to the right at a left-hand bend. The forest trail traverses the northern slopes of the main ridge; giant fern fronds encroach the path. After almost half an hour, several paths branch off (to the left, a possible ascent to Pijaral) but we remain on the main trail which bears to the right descending to the road; now follow the road by turning right. Those who want to avoid walking along the road as much as possible can do so by taking subsequent forest trails branching off to the left and right. Either way, it takes about half an hour (at the end passing a youth hostel) to return to **El Bailadero**.

38 Montaña Tafada, 606 m

Peaceful mountain hike with some athletic interludes

Chamorga – Montaña Tafada (– Faro de Anaga) – Chamorga

Starting point: Chamorga, 500 m, at the end of the Anaga mountain road (bus stop for line 247).

Walking times: Chamorga – house at Montaña Tafada 1¼ hrs, house – Montaña Tafada ¼ hr, Montaña Tafada – Chamorga almost 1 hr; total time 2½ hrs.

Ascent: About 250 m.

Grade: Mostly good trails and paths, however some stretches are somewhat exposed.

Refreshment: Bar in Chamorga.

Alternative: Descent to Faro de Anaga, 230 m (¾ hr one way): In front of the house at Montaña Tafada, turn left onto the trail and down through the barren northern slopes of Montaña Tafada soon enjoying a pretty view of the coast and the lighthouse. The path, sometimes somewhat exposed, heads over to a mountain ridge and then descends steeply to Faro de Anaga (a few minutes before the lighthouse, a trail from El Draguillo merges from the left).

Combination possible with Walks 37 and 39.

The surroundings of the picturesquely situated village of Chamorga presents an eldorado for walkers. Beautiful old cobblestone trails and paths traverse the laurisilva forests and frequently open magnificent views of the coast – this is just the case of this not-quite-so spectacular, but nevertheless entertaining walk. If you wish to extend the tour, we recommend taking an excursion from Montaña Tafada to the Faro de Anaga.

Directly in front of the church of **Chamorga** follow the cement track ascending sharply to the left (*Camino La Rosalta*) but leave it a short time later by taking the *camino* that continues straight ahead along a brook. After a good 10 min reach a fork on the left side of the valley then bear right (from the left, a trail merges from La Cumbrilla). The congenial trail now leads back to the valley floor, crosses the brook and ascends on the right flank of the valley to a trail junction on the ridgeline of the Anaga main ridge (total time ½ hr); here, bear

The abandoned farmstead on Montaña Tafada.

right. At first the trail ascends steeply, often opening breathtaking downward views of the coast between El Draguillo and Almáciga. Some minutes later, the trail traverses the slope to the right of the ridge for a while. At the striking rocky »finger« of **Roque Icoso**, the trail returns again to the ridgeline – far below, we can see the nearly abandoned hamlet of Las Palmas as well as the Roques de Anaga. Afterwards, other beautiful views of Chamorga open up. 20 min after passing Roque Icoso, reach a saddle, 597 m, on the ridgeline trail with an abandoned property – about 75 m before the house, a trail merges sharply from the right coming from Chamorga (our return route later on).

In front of the house, the trail forks: the main trail leads to the left descending to Faro de Anaga (→Alternative) however, we bear to the right continuing over the mountain ridge to the crest of **Montaña Tafada**, 593 m (¼ hr), which plunges steeply to the east. From here, enjoy a fantastic downwards view of Roques de Anaga, Roque Bermejo and Faro de Anaga.

Now walk back to the house on the saddle in front of Montaña Tafada and, about 75 m on, take the left turn at the fork (about 50 m before the scrub wood) onto a slightly ascending trail. From time to time, a few short rocky stretches must be mastered. After about 20 min, the route ascends gently to a saddle next to a rock spur then takes a sharp right descending sometimes over rock. At the »Casa Alvaro« (bar with a small grocery store next to it) the trail merges into the village street of **Chamorga**; turn right here and head back to the starting point.

39 Grand Faro de Anaga Circuit

Spectacular, strenuous circuit walk in the extreme north-east of Tenerife

Chamorga – El Draguillo – Las Palmas – Faro de Anaga – Roque Bermejo – Chamorga

Starting point: Chamorga, 500 m, at the end of the Anaga mountain road (bus stop for line 247).

Walking times: Chamorga – El Draguillo 1¼ hrs, El Draguillo – Las Palmas ¾ hr, Las Palmas – Faro de Anaga 1 hr, Faro de Anaga – Roque Bermejo ½ hr, Roque Bermejo – Chamorga 1¼ hrs, total time 4¾ hrs (when beginning the circuit at Playa de San Roque, add 2½ hrs).

Ascent: About 1100 m.

Grade: Strenuous circuit walk on somewhat precipitous trails; constant ascents and descents.

Refreshment: Bar in Chamorga.

Alternative: From Roque de las Bodegas at Playa de San Roque near Almáciga to El Draguillo (1¼ hrs): From

Playa de San Roque (bus stop for line 246) follow the coastal road to the east. Some minutes later, the village road of Almáciga branches off to the right; ¼ hr later, pass the Playa de Benijo (small sand beach with two beach houses; dangerous undertow). If the surf allows, you can continue walking from there directly along the coast (to El Draguillo) – otherwise, stay on the asphalt road that now ascends to Benijo (½ hr; bar/restaurant). 100 m after the sign for the village limits, a track road turns off to the left, passes the restaurant »El Frontón« and then leaves the hamlet. This leads high above the coast, at times ascending steeply, and reaches El Draguillo in a good half hour.

Combination possible with Walks 35–38.

The walk around the north-eastern tip of Tenerife, with its isolated, still mostly unspoilt villages and numerous offshore islands (remnant volcanic cones) is one of the greatest walking tours of Tenerife, however, due to its length and the differences in elevation (which should not be taken lightly) this route can only be recommended for mountain hikers with plenty of stamina. You can also begin the tour in Roque de las Bodegas – then, however, the walk is extended by over two hours to make a total of about seven hours!

Surrounded by rocky mountains, **Chamorga** is delightfully nestled in the ever-verdant valley head of Barranco de Roque Bermejo and, next to Masca, is considered one of the most beautifully situated villages on the island. The Anaga mountain road, directly at the village limits, ends at the church. Across from the church, turn sharply to the left onto a cement trail heading uphill (Camino La Rosalta) leaving this shortly after by following a *camino* straight on. The *camino* leads along a brook through a romantic valley and then ascends, bearing left, into the laurel wood. After a good 10 min, at a turn-off, bear right (from the left, a path merges from La Cumbrilla). Soon cross the

View from Cabezo del Tejo to the west – on the right, Almáciga.

brook and, on the right side of the valley, ascend to a saddle on the ridgeline of the Anaga main ridge to reach a trail junction (signs; ½ hr).

To the left, one could take a short but demanding excursion to Cabezo del Tejo, 750 m, one of the most breathtaking panoramic overlooks on the island (a good 10 min one way) however, we continue from the saddle straight on

View from Las Palmas to Roque de Dentro.

and begin a descent on the other side of the ridge. The path leads downward in steep zigzags and after 20 min the laurel wood thins – the picturesquely situated hamlet **El Draguillo**, 170 m, appears below. Descend between terraces, the first ones overgrown with disuse but those further on are cultivated, into the hamlet and pass a dragon tree on a track (to the left, this leads to Almáciga in a good hour).

Before the trail merges with the track, a walking trail branches off to the right. This immediately passes through a *barranco* gully then ascends traversing the slope above the coast. Soon, cross two fields of scree one after the other dropping steeply and dangerously toward the sea then the next destination of the walk appears – the isolated hamlet of Las Palmas, situated on a verdant mountain promontory in front of the Roques de Anaga. The coastal trail initially ascends to an altitude of not quite 300 m. Only shortly before reaching **Las Palmas**, 150 m, does it descend steeply in zigzags into an overgrown *barranco* and past prickly pear cactus (Opuntias) growing over two metres high, to reach the first house of the pristine, romantic and almost completely abandoned hamlet.

If you wish, you can take a side trip to the right into the hamlet with its overgrown gardens, however, we continue on the coastal trail to reach a fork at the opposite end of the hamlet – across from us, the mighty, 178-metre high Roque de Dentro towers out of the sea. Our route continues straight ahead, crosses a *barranco* and then ascends steadily. After 20 min, pass a giant, curious-looking boulder with stone houses built into it and a grape press (Las Orobales). Ascend steeply for a short stretch then the trail traverses the slope in easy up-and-down walking. Almost ½ hr later, pass a picnic place with a table and benches situated at the foot of a massive rock cliff. There is a small shrine built into the cliff and next to it is an enclosed spring (Fuente del Junquillo). Now take only a quarter hour to reach **Faro de Anaga**, 230 m (along the way, a trail merges from the right descending from Montaña Tafada, →Walk 38).

From the lighthouse, continue a descent along the broad and sometimes slide-damaged trail towards Roque Bermejo (signposted). After 20 min reach a major, signposted trail crossing. To the right, our route continues to Chamorga but first, we recommend an excursion (straight on) to **Roque Bermejo** – the trail passes the houses and the chapel of the hamlet descending to a narrow strip of sand beach with a few fishermen's huts. In the adjoining northern bay, the port and Roque Bermejo are located.

Back at the trail crossing, follow the hiking trail in the direction of Chamorga. This ascends between gardens then over a mountain ridge to a lone, dilapidated house and finally ascends along a telegraph line on the edge of the impressive, chasm-like Barranco de Roque Bermejo. After 40 min, skirt around a mountain spur and a few minutes later pass a first house. Between gardens (to the right and above, you can see a small dragon tree grove) the trail becomes a gravel road. This brings us past the bar »Casa Alvaro‹ and a little grocery store (the road is now asphalt) into **Chamorga** and back to the church – our starting point.

The fishing village of Roque Bermejo and beyond it the rock tower of the same name.

40 From Igueste to Las Casillas

Ascent above the Barranco de Igueste to an abandoned mountain village

Igueste de San Andrés – Lomo Bermejo – Las Casillas – Anaga mountain road and back

Starting point: Turn-off of the access road into the Barranco de Igueste in Igueste de San Andrés, 30 m (last bus stop for line 245). If you approach by car, you can drive up to Lomo Bermejo.

Walking times: Igueste – Lomo Bermejo ½ hr, Lomo Bermejo – Las Casillas 1½ hrs, Las Casillas – Anaga mountain road ½ hr, return route 2 hrs; total time 4½ hrs.

Ascent: A good 600 m.

Grade: Sometimes steep ascents and descents; orientation may be problematic in periods of poor visibility.

Refreshment: Bar/restaurant at the village limits of Igueste; from there a trail descends to the lovely beach.

Alternative: Continued route from the Anaga mountain road to Chamorga: 20 m after the turn-off of the street to the cemetery, a *camino* forks off to the right from the main road only to return to it again 5 min later. Take the main road to the right (after a few minutes, bear left at the fork) up to the road tunnel of La Cumbrilla (10 min). Turn left here via the stepped trail up to the houses on the top of the ridgeline. To the left, past the shrine, a cobblestone path continues the route. This enters a cloud forest and forks a few minutes later. Here, either to the right descending to the road (¼ hr to Chamorga)

or diagonally to the left, retaining the same elevation and after 15 min bear right at the fork descending to Chamorga (total ½ or ¾ hr).

From Chamorga, several route extensions are possible (→Walks 37–39).

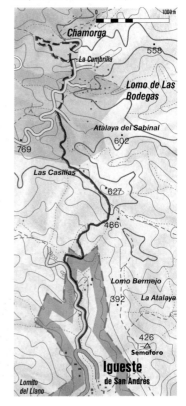

The destination of this walk is the pristine and romantic mountain eyrie of Las Casillas perched on the ridgeline of the ridge between the Barrancos de Igueste and Ijuana. The hamlet is practically abandoned; only a dragon tree and two cedars are reminders of better times.

Igueste, the starting point of the hike, as seen from Atalaya de los Ingleses.

From the end of the street in **Igueste** return on the main road back to the sharp bend between the two village districts; here, turn right onto a road which ascends into the Barranco de Igueste. Cross through plantations for a while and then pass the houses of the hamlet **Lomo Bermejo**. After a good half hour, directly below a mighty, hollowed crag in the middle of the *barranco*, a stepped trail forks off to the right (sign »*Las Casillas*«).

The pretty *camino* crosses a small tributary *barranco* then forks soon after – bear left here. Between cultivated terraces and again crossing the tributary *barranco*, the trail leads to the left towards the ridge then ascends along it. Almost half an hour from the road, reach a gentle saddle next to a small rock tower. The path now skirts around to the right of a few boulders on the ridgeline but soon returns to the ridgeline where it then forks – bear left, ascending steeply. Now steadily onwards to the mountain promontory before us from which our mountain ridge drops down. Just below the crest oft the mountain promontory, we can see a power line – about 50 m below this, the trail forks once again and here again bear left (to the right, a possible descent to Playa de Antequera). The trail now ascends to the crest (reach this exactly at the spot where the power line turns away from the crest). Here bear left and 20 min later reach the houses of **Las Casillas**, 610 m.

Between the houses, the ridge trail continues but soon leads into the valley to the right of the ridgeline. On the other side, exit the valley once again and soon pass a house built into an overhanging cliff. Traverse another valley cleft then the trail ascends for a short stretch steeply up to the **Anaga mountain road**, 645 m (merging directly at the turn-off of the access road for the cemetery of Las Bodegas; sign »*Igueste*«).

41 From Igueste to Playa de Antequera

Multifarious coastal walk to the delightful Antequera Beach

Igueste de San Andrés – Atalaya de los Ingleses (– Ensenada de Zapata) – Playa de Antequera and back

Starting point: End of the main road in Igueste de San Andrés, 30 m (last bus stop for line 245).

Walking times: Igueste – Atalaya de los Ingleses 1 hr, Atalaya de los Ingleses – Ensenada de Zapata almost 1 hr, Ensenada de Zapata – Playa de Antequera ½ hr, return route 2½ hrs; total time 5 hrs.

Ascent: A total of 1000 m.

Grade: Moderately difficult tour that requires some sure-footedness, a head for heights and a good sense of direction. This walk should not be undertaken in rainy or stormy weather.

Refreshment: Bar/restaurant in Igueste.

Alternative: Return route through Barranco de Antequera (2¾ hrs): At the end of the sand beach, ascend to the left along the trail that leads past a few houses. At the second (little) building, a *camino* branches off to the right. The trail, not always distinct, steadily follows the Barranco de Antequera, changing valley sides several times and after 1¼ hrs passes beneath a light-coloured, long cliff wall on the left flank of the valley. Some minutes later, reach the ridge. The trail now follows the ridgeline for a few metres then turns toward the left side of the ridge and finally forks after 50 m. Here, bear to the left onto the slightly descending trail and at the next fork under a power line ascend to the right over rock steps and then cross over to the next mountain ridge to meet up with a *camino* (to the right, a possible ascent to Las Casillas, →Walk 40). Descend along the *camino* and in 40 min reach the road in the Barranco de Igueste; follow the road back to Igueste in ½ hr.

Stretches of this walk require some forbearance since the trail is often indistinct; a head for heights is also necessary during the somewhat exposed traverse above the coast towards Antequera Beach. You will be rewarded, however, with a good dose of romantic adventure as well as a beautiful beach at the end.

Follow the footpath continuing from the end of the main road in **Igueste** into the village. At a fork past the church take the upper trail, soon passing a small radio tower then keep straight on towards the sea. After a total of a good 5 min, a wide *camino* branches off to the left before a railing (arrow drawn on the footpath; straight on leads to the cemetery) then ascends steeply in zig-

A most desirable destination during the exposed traverse – Antequera Beach.

zags. A quarter hour later, the trail passes a rock spur (a small overlook plateau). 20 min later reach the ocean side of the mountain ridge. Now pay close attention: after about 15 m on the ocean side, a distinct rock path branches off to the left, traversing the slope and crossing inland to ascend to the ridge. The path is somewhat precipitous in spots but nevertheless easy to walk along. After a walking time of almost 1 hr reach the ridgeline at a cairn then continue ascending the ridge bearing to the left with hardly a trace of a path to reach **Atalaya de los Ingleses**, 429 m, with an old, chapel-like stone house.

The path continues to the right past the house – the descent into the next slope is to the right of the ridgeline of our mountain ridge and is clearly marked by large cairns. The path first descends in a 10-min traverse of the slope below the rocks then turns sharply to the right at a cairn onto a sometimes indistinct path that leads down into the valley. After a good 10 min, the cairn-marked path switches to the right flank of the *barranco* then 10 min later back to the left flank. The trail forks 3 min later – bear left traversing the slope in easy up-and-down walking. Almost 10 min later, pass an overhanging rock (rest spot). After 5 more min, just before a gully, take a left at the fork (to the right a possible descent to the tiny Zapata Beach) and shortly after cross the gully. 5 min after the gully crossing, the narrow, precipitous path passes below a rock tower. The most unpleasant part of the walk then follows – the good quarter-hour traverse to Antequera Bay: this crosses high above the sea and is sometimes somewhat exposed. As soon as we approach the rim of Barranco de Antequera, descend along the mountain ridge, then to the right of it along the slope, to finally reach the long **Antequera Beach**, finishing the route directly next to the mouth of the *barranco*.

42 From Pico del Inglés to Santa Cruz

On an old mountain path from the Anaga main ridge to the island's capital

Pico del Inglés – Cabeza del Viento – Tahodío – Barrio de la Alegría

Starting point: Mirador Pico del Inglés, 992 m (bus stop for line 073).
Destination: Barrio de la Alegría (Santa Cruz), 10 m, on the highway between Santa Cruz and San Andrés (several bus lines).
Walking times: Pico del Inglés – 2nd farmstead a good 1 hr, continued descent to Barrio de la Alegría 1½ hrs; total time 2½ hrs (return route 2¾ hrs).
Descent: 1000 m.
Grade: Easy walk via an old trail connecting villages.
Refreshment: In Santa Cruz.
Alternative: If you prefer a circuit walk (total time 2½ hrs; 3¾ hrs including excursion to Casa Santiago), turn left at the second farmstead on the route to Degollada de las Hijas. After ¼ hr, the trail reaches the ridgeline (houses) then leads straight on traversing the slope. After 10 min cross over a gentle saddle; a good 5 min later continue straight ahead at the fork ascending along the slope (the right fork offers a descent to Catalanes). After ¼ hr, the trail enters a scrub wood; a good 5 min later meet up with the approach route that ascends to the right in 25 min to Mirador Pico del Inglés. – Half way along this route (after almost 15 min and 10 min before the *mirador*) a trail to the right offers a lovely, somewhat adventurous excursion to Degollada de las Hijas (sign): after 3 min, at the fork, do not bear left over the ridge but instead continue on the right side of the ridge passing below the Roque de la Fortaleza. Not quite 10 min later remain left on the narrow, precipitous

path below the cliff face. After a good 5 min, the path crosses over to the right of the ridge then a few minutes later arrives at a T-junction in a scrub wood. To the right, the trail descends in a good 10 min to the bar/restaurant »Casa Santiago« on the Anaga mountain road (Casas de la Cumbre, bus stop for lines 076, 077); to the left, the trail turns back towards Mirador Pico del Inglés. After a good 5 min, the trail merges into an abandoned road; here ascend for 10 min until reaching a distinct trail junction. Turn sharply left onto the trail, ascending along power pylons and after 5 min take a sharp right at a fork to reach Mirador Pico del Inglés in 5 min.

The scenic overlook Mirador Pico del Inglés offers one of the most beautiful vistas of Tenerife: vast stretches of the northern island lay before us and the neighbouring island of Gran Canaria appears to be only a stone's throw away. An ancient trail leads from here down to Santa Cruz. At the end of the walk, enjoy a stroll through the streets of the capital or an excursion to Playa de las Teresitas.

The walk begins at the end of the street to the left of **Mirador Pico del Inglés** (sign *»Barrio de la Alegría«*). Descend for 5 min in a southerly direction through a dense laurel wood until reaching a fork (a good 50 m after passing a dilapidated building). Here, remain to the right of the mountain ridge and 5 min later at another fork continue straight on (the trail to the left leads to Degollada de las Hijas, →Alternative). A good 5 min later, pass a stone house; in not quite another 5 min reach a trail junction – here continue straight ahead on the middle trail. Immediately after, bear left at a fork (below the trail and to the right – a superbly-formed group of crags compliment a splendid view towards Teide).

The path now veers away from the ridgeline of **Cabeza del Viento** and descends in zigzags bearing right. Sadly, we also leave the laurel wood behind. A good half hour after the junction reach a marvellously located farmstead with a threshing yard and a couple of caves used for keeping animals. The hiking trail continues to the right of the threshing yard and after a good 10 min arrives at a second farmstead. Below the house, the path forks – bear right here (to the left – *»Degollada de las Hijas«*, →Alternative).

The further descent to **Barrio de la Alegría** leads down to the right to the small Barranco de Valle Luis, switches to the right side of the slope and then descends along the stream bed, repeatedly changing sides of the valley – a beautiful, tranquil descent over meadow terraces, past fig trees and partly overgrown, partly tended gardens. After almost 1 hr, the cobblestone trail merges with the asphalt road at the base of Barranco de Tahodío. Follow this to the left through a hopelessly ravaged valley landscape until reaching the coastal highway Santa Cruz–San Andrés (3 km, a good ½ hr).

The Cañadas del Teide

Wide sand plains, bizarre rocks and a white sugar loaf mountain

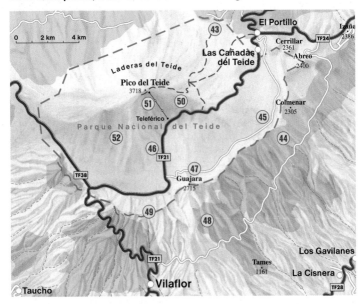

The national park »Parque Nacional de las Cañadas del Teide« is the main attraction of the island, drawing millions of visitors annually; a normally cloudless sky presents a weighty argument for holidaymakers sojourning in the north of the island who only seldom enjoy a break in the clouds brought in by the trade winds. The sand and lava terrain at the southern foot of Teide, with sparse vegetation and characterised by bizarre rock formations and volcanic cones, guarantees lasting impressions. In early summer (May/June), the volcanic landscape of the Cañadas is covered in a sea of rare flora. White-blossoming Teide broom, bright golden-yellow budding common broom and other varieties envelop the area with a captivating fragrance; to top it off, the candle-like floral crowns of the Teide »tower of jewels«, stretching up to two metres high, and countless other plants only found in the caldera compete for the attention of pollen-collecting bees. Some plants just flower for a few hours or days and then the land is once again coloured by a desert-like character, reminiscent of a lunar landscape.

A view from Guajara of Teide and Montaña Blanca with La Palma in the background.

The caldera was formed about 300,000 years ago through the collapse of a mighty volcanic cone, out of whose floor the Pico del Teide, Pico Viejo and numerous other volcanic mountains formed in subsequent eruptions. The so-called »Sugar Loaf« (Pan de Azucár or Pitón) – the white peak of Teide above Rambleta (here the summit terminus of the Teide cable car can be found) – is of more recent volcanic origin; in this area, puffs of sulphurous gas still emerge from the depths of the mountain.

STARTING POINTS FOR WALKS

El Portillo, 2050 m

Traffic junction at km 32 of the Cañadas mountain road, at the north-east edge of the Cañadas. Bar/restaurant and National Park Visitor Centre (Centro de Visitantes; with an exhibit explaining the creation of the Cañadas and information on walking trails). Walking trails to Fortaleza, Montaña Blanca and the southern rim of the crater.

Teleférico del Teide, 2356 m

Valley terminus of the Teide cable car, at km 42.5 on the Cañadas road. Starting point for the Teide ascent (actual starting point 3 km to the east).

Parador Nacional de las Cañadas, 2150 m

State-owned hotel and National Park Visitor Centre at km 46.5 of Cañadas road. Ideal base for any tour in the Cañadas (accommodation available) and the starting point for walks to the Roques de García and Guajara, among others.

Boca Tauce, 2055 m

Road intersection at km 53 of the Cañadas road at the south-western rim of the Cañadas. Starting point for tours to the caldera crater rim and Pico Viejo.

43 Risco de la Fortaleza, 2159 m

Introducing the region with a walk to the rock »fortification«

El Portillo – Roque del Peral – Cañada de los Guancheros – Choza Cruz de Fregel – Risco de la Fortaleza and back

Starting point: Centro de Visitantes (National Park Visitor Centre) in El Portillo, 2050 m, 250 m past the traffic junction at the bar/restaurant »El Portillo« (bus stop for lines 342/348).
Walking times: El Portillo – Roque del Peral 20 min, Roque del Peral – Choza Cruz de Fregel 1 hr, Choza Cruz de Fregel – Risco de la Fortaleza ¼ hr, return route

1¼ hrs; total time almost 3 hrs.
Ascent: Almost 200 m.
Grade: With the exception of the pathless summit ascent, a consistently easy and pleasant walk.
Refreshment: Bar/restaurant »El Portillo«.
Alternative: From Choza Cruz de Fregel, descent possible to Mirador La Corona (→Walk 12).

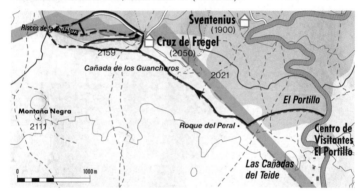

If you would like to get acquainted with the marvellous walking terrain of the Cañadas, the route to the Fortaleza (»fortification«) is the ideal choice. Begin with a worthwhile visit to the Centro des Visitantes (Visitor Centre) where a small, informative exhibit on the geology, flora and fauna of Teide National Park can be found. The walk leads through gentle hills of lava and sand on the northern edge of the Cañadas, broken up by sprinklings of common broom and Teide broom flowering in early summer. At the end of the walk, the reddish-brown rocky massif of Fortaleza and a pretty, tree-shaded picnic area await us.

Our walking trail begins directly to the left of the **Centro de Visitantes** (National Park Visitor Centre). This passes below a small vista point then through a gate in the fence to continue towards Teide in steady up-and-down walking. Initially the trail is flanked with lines of stones and from time to time, stone

Fortaleza, to the right the saddle of Degollada del Cedro.

benches tempt us to take a break. After a quarter hour, on a small plain, the trail forks – continue straight on (not to the right; at the fork 50 m further, once again continue straight on). 5 min later, somewhat below **Roque del Peral**, the trail merges with an intersecting trail which we follow to the right. This trail leads around the group of rocks and then heads toward the rocky ridge of Fortaleza in gentle up-and-down walking. Near the foot of Cabezón (»the Stubborn One«), the trail leads down into an extensive, beige-coloured sand plain, the **Cañada de los Guancheros**.

Cross the plain towards the west (you could also ascend to the Cruz de Fregel by climbing directly to the right) and after 10 min turn sharply to the right at the end of the plain onto the distinct trail that ascends somewhat beneath the rock cliff of Fortaleza (if you walked for a good 5 min more on the path continuing straight on, you would reach a drop-off with a marvellous view of the north-western coast; the trail leads further down to La Guancha and La Corona). Several »tower of jewels« plants can be found on the slope at the foot of the rock wall. After a quarter hour and just past a barrier, reach the beautifully situated picnic area **Cruz de Fregel** (barbecue sites, tables and benches, small chapel) in Degollada del Cedro (»Cedar Saddle«).

Now follow the gently ascending track to the left which ends soon after passing a shrine. Now bear to the left, without a distinct path, and climb to the highest point of **Fortaleza** – the view stretches from Teide to the vast forests of the Orotava Valley.

The descent route follows the ascent route, although a direct descent can be made from Cruz de Fregel to Cañada de los Guancheros.

44 Cañadas Mountain Trail – from El Portillo to Parador Nacional

Mountain trail on the caldera rim – only for the physically fit hiker

El Portillo – Degollada de Abreo – Pasajirón – Degollada de Guajara – Parador Nacional

Starting point: Centro de Visitantes in El Portillo, 2050 m, 250 m after the road intersection at the bar/restaurant »El Portillo« (bus stop for lines 342/348).

Destination: Parador Nacional, 2150 m (bus stop for lines 342/348).

Walking times: El Portillo – Degollada de Abreo 1¾ hrs, Degollada de Abreo – Montaña Pasajirón 3 hrs, Montaña Pasajirón – Parador 1¼ hrs; total time 6 hrs.

Ascent: About 600 m and 500 m in descent.

Grade: With the exception of the ascent and descent to Montaña Pasajirón, consistently uncomplicated but strenuous walk.

Refreshment: At the starting point, the bar/restaurant »El Portillo«, at the destination, the hotel »Parador Nacional de las Cañadas«.

Combination possible with Walks 45 and 47.

The mountain trail from El Portillo to the summit of Pasajirón is by no means one of the grand routes of the island, nevertheless, the route usu-

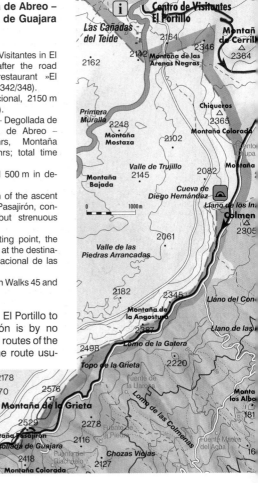

ally follows tracks that frequently offer magnificent panoramas of the Cañadas and Teide and, in periods of good visibility, vast stretches of the south-east coast.

Across from the **Centro de Visitantes** (National Park Visitor Centre) a forestry road begins at a barrier then forks after just 5 min. Follow the left track (small sign »*Sendero 2*«), ascending in wide bends. After half an hour, antennas and the observatory of Izaña come into view. Passing through a hollow, continue up to the broad saddle between Montaña de las Arenas Negras and Montaña Cerrillar (a total of 1 hr). Now we have Teide and Guajara in view. Remain on the gently descending track along the slope and soon cross an extensive sand plain, the Llano de Maja (at a fork to the right, continue straight on) following the traces of a track. Half an hour after the broad saddle meet up with a dirt road behind a sand mound and continue along this to the right (south). About 10 min later, a track branches off to the right to the panoramic Montaña de las Piedras (¼ hr one way) however, walk straight on along the main track and shortly after reach the gentle saddle **Degollada de Abreo**, 2314 m (wooden cross).

Here the track bends slightly to the right and leads down into a vast mountain plateau. Passing a military training area and later the black, sand hill of Montaña Colmenas lying to our left, reach after 1 hr (from Degollada de Abreo) a gentle saddle near the rim of the caldera – continue straight on here (sign »*Sin Salida*«). The track diverges somewhat away from the ridgeline and after almost half an hour reaches a saddle with a view of the Cañadas and Teide. 20 min later, reach another saddle. Subsequently, the now increasingly bumpy track ascends in a few bends then continues in a pleasant traverse of a slope. After 45 min, passing a large pine, reach a valley gap descending from the saddle between Roque de la Grieta and the Pasajirón.

Here, pay close attention: about 10 m after the gentle valley floor, a distinct path forks off to the right (large white arrow on boulders at the trail's edge). The path bears mostly to the left, climbing steeply through the broom-blanketed slope (watch out for white/green markings) and after about 15 min passes between two small rock cliffs. High up on the summit plateau, the path continues far to the left of the ridgeline – also the highest point of **Montaña Pasajirón**, 2527 m (a good ½ hr after the fork in the path) is skirted to the left by traversing the slope.

Now the path descends bearing to the right and after 5 min reaches the ridgeline. Descending along this – sometimes a little below the ridge to the left – reach **Guajara-Pass**, 2372 m. From here, ascend along the ridge for about 3 min until reaching a large cairn (50 m before beige-coloured crags) marking a distinct trail descending to the Cañadas track (20 min). Take a left onto this and after 40 min, passing Piedras Amarillas at the end, reach an asphalt road; follow this to the right and on to the main road. Take a right onto this and head to the nearby **Parador**.

45 Cañadas Track – from Parador Nacional to El Portillo

Easy walk along the foot of the caldera cliffs

Parador Nacional – Cañada de la Grieta – Cañada de las Pilas – El Portillo

Starting point: Parador Nacional, 2150 m (bus stop for lines 342/348).

Destination: El Portillo, 2050 m (bus stop for lines 342/348).

Walking times: Parador Nacional – turn-off of the track to the Teide cable car almost 1 hr, turn-off – Cañada de la Grieta ¾ hr, Cañada de la Grieta – turn-off Las Cañadas del Teide 2¼ hrs, turn-off – El Portillo ¼ hr; total time 4¼ hrs.

Ascent: Only short ascents (200 m) and descents (300 m).

Grade: Easy, but long walk on a consistently wide track.

Refreshment: Hotel/restaurant »Parador« and bar/restaurant »El Portillo«.

Alternatives: If you find the walking route to El Portillo too long, you can turn off after almost 1 hr onto the track leading to the Teide cable car: This leads past a former sanatorium (20 min) to the Cañadas main road (1 hr); from here it takes only another 15 min to reach the valley terminus.

Combination possible with Walk 44.

This pleasant walk leads along the edge of the Cañadas to El Portillo, passing between gigantic fields of lava and the impressive cliff walls of the caldera rim – a tranquil ramble.

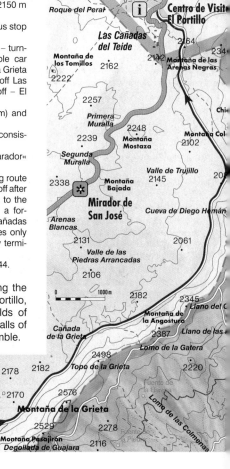

Well worth the detour – the former sanatorio with a view of Teide.

From **Parador Nacional**, follow the main road for a short time in the direction of Vilaflor and, at the sign »*Los Roques*«, turn left onto a street which ends at a barrier near a little stone hut of the national park administration (15 min).

Bearing to the left, a gravel track continues which skirts around the bizarre cluster of rocks **Piedras Amarillas** (»Yellow Rocks«). A little further on, pass another group of crags. After 40 min – shortly before, a track branches off to the left which leads to the valley terminus of the Teide cable car – reach the edge of an extended plain, and now pass below Montaña Pasajirón. Pass a beautiful crag cluster then head gently downhill along the foot of Roque de la Grieta into a gully bordered on the left by a mighty lava flow – several »tower of jewels« plants grow along the sun-bathed slopes. At the foot of Topo de la Grieta, the track descends further to a rather large alluvial plain, the **Cañada de la Grieta** – traces of another track branch off to the left but we remain on our track which now ascends gently. Further along, the scenery becomes more and more monotonous. After 45 min, reach a vast plain, the **Cañada de las Pilas**; on the other side of the plain (a good ½ hr) pass between boulders and along a towering crag. On the next plain, enjoy the fascinating, colourful layers and formations in the cliff walls. At the end of the plain (just under ½ hr) the track takes a hook. Another small plain follows and, 100 m on, a path branches off to the left, leading to the nearby restaurants of Las Cañadas del Teide. Continue along the track passing a barrier after 10 min and shortly after reach the Centro de Visitantes in **El Portillo** on the main road.

46 Roques de García

Unforgettable circuit route around the most bizarre crags of the Cañadas

Mirador de la Ruleta – Roques de García – Catedral – Los Azulejos – Mirador de la Ruleta

Starting point: Parador Nacional de las Cañadas, 2150 m (bus stop for lines 342/348) or the car park at Mirador de la Ruleta, at the foot of Roques de García.
Walking times: Mirador de la Ruleta – vista plateau ½ hr, vista plateau – Catedral ½ hr, Catedral – Mirador de la Ruleta ¾ hr; total time 1¾ hrs.
Ascent: 150 m.
Grade: Mostly easy walk on trails and paths.
Refreshment: In the hotel »Parador Nacional«.
Combination possible with Walk 47.

The Roques de García, situated in the heart of the Cañadas at the foot of Teide, present what is probably the island's most beautiful natural monument. Especially Roque Cinchado, the so-called »Finger of God«, attracts swarms of tourists and day trippers. It takes just a few minutes, however, for the walker to be immersed in the stillness of the Cañadas, so that he can concentrate on discovering for himself the fantastic natural wonders around this bizarre, multi-dimensional rock massif.

The Catedral.

From the roundabout at **Mirador de la Ruleta**, walk along the right edge of the barrier, passing beneath the »Finger of God«. After only a few minutes reach a small saddle at the end of the barrier. Here, bear right and follow the path which runs along the foot of the next group of crags. After about 15 min, a lava flow encroaches from the right extending toward the crags which are sometimes perforated with holes – similar to *tafoni* rock formations. About 10 min later, reach the last, solitary crag tower of the Roques de García. Pass this to the right and reach a small **vista plateau** at the precipice

Roques de García – a very popular »city of crags«.

dropping off to the Llano de Ucanca plain (nice spot to take a break).
Circumventing the small group of rocks that follows, descend in the direction
of the Ucanca plain, bearing left. – If you like, after the short descent, you can
then ascend to the right along the lava flow, however, we descend into the
small valley to the left of this. Cairns guide us along the best route which follows along the right edge of the small valley. After about 20 min, arrive at the
foot of a mighty, multiple-peaked rock formation. Continue at its foot down to
the Ucanca plain, directly toward the **Catedral** (up on the crest, the »Finger of
God« appears again). The roughly 100-m high rock bastion displays several
striking towers and looks quite like a cathedral – from time to time, you can see
climbers clinging to the steep walls.
If you prefer, you can return to Mirador de la Ruleta to the left on the steep
path, however, we go right, around the Catedral passing a rock formation rid-
dled with holes then cross the Ucanca plain to reach its eastern edge. Here, a
small path ascends to the left to the blue-green coloured rocks of **Azulejos**.
After a short ascent, the path crosses a gully. On the left edge of the blue-
green coloured field of scree, climb up to the nearby Cañadas road and turning left onto it, arrive back at the starting point.

47 Guajara, 2715 m

A paragon of a panoramic mountain with adventurous routes

Parador Nacional – Piedras Amarillas – Degollada de Guajara – Guajara – Degollada de Ucanca – Piedras Amarillas – Parador Nacional

Starting point: Parador Nacional de las Cañadas, 2150 m (bus stop for lines 342/348).

Walking times: Parador – Guajara Pass 1½ hrs, Guajara Pass – Guajara 1 hr, Guajara – Ucanca Pass 1 hr, Ucanca Pass – Parador almost 1 hr; total time 4½ hrs.

Ascent: 600 m.

Grade: The ascent is easy to moderate, the descent is exposed in some spots. During periods of poor visibility, expect possible orientation problems.

Refreshment: In the hotel »Parador Nacional«.

Alternative: Descent from Guajara Pass to the lunar landscape (Paisaje Lunar): Follow the described route to the iron rod and from there continue straight on along the trail at the edge of Barranco del Río. The distinct path leads in a slight ascent to a mountain ridge and then traverses to the right to the neighbouring *barranco* – here, too, a path branches off to the right to the summit of Guajara. Head straight on and cross the small *barranco* – along its edge, the route heads further downhill then the path bears more to the right toward the brownish-black shimmering mound of volcanic scoria – Montaña de las Arenas. The path now leads in bends along a mountain ridge down to a wide, gently downwards sloping sandy landscape – after ½ hr (from the iron rod) reach the sand ridge and walk straight on down this following a row of stones, enjoying a great view of the southern coast and the »black lunar landscape« to the right. Shortly before the end of the sand slope and before reaching the first pines, bear to the right to descend into Barranco de las Arenas (you could also continue straight on but you would see very little of the Paisaje Lunar), cross the *barranco* and ascend along the path to the left to the next mountain ridge. From here, the trail drops gently and after a few minutes reaches a small rocky plateau where we have our first look at the lunar landscape. 50 m further on, a distinctly marked path forks left into the sandy terrain. In a straight line, continue through a steep sand gully with young pines, descending almost 200 m in elevation toward the lunar landscape. Arriving here, keep left following the path over to the next sand gully and continue descending along the path through a small *barranco* to the foot of the upper group of rocks of the lunar landscape. The green-marked path leads further down into the *barranco* between the two groups of rocks (up to this point, a total of almost 1½ hrs from Guajara Pass). Now, go either further down to the dirt road (→Walk 48) or back to the Guajara Pass (a good 1¾ hrs, →Walk 48).

Guajara with the Parador and the Piedras Amarillas. The descent route is clear to see – below the summit face, descending to the right to Ucanca Pass.

The broad-shouldered Guajara is not only the highest but also the most striking mountain formation of the extensive circle of the caldera peaks. Not only offering a pleasant mountain experience, it also allows the walker the enjoyment of a magnificent panorama of Teide, the Cañadas and the neighbouring islands of Gran Canaria, El Hierro, La Gomera and La Palma. In addition, countless »tower of jewels« plants grow on its sun-bathed slopes, in early summer blooming in luxuriant floral display.

From the Parador Nacional, two routes lead up to the summit: our ascent follows the more popular route, which can be undertaken by any walker; the descent route follows the wide, sometimes somewhat exposed, rocky ledges which (as seen from the Parador) lead down below the summit to the Ucanca Pass – if you do not feel comfortable with this rather precipitous route, you can return to the starting point via the ascent route (2 hrs). Of course, we cannot fail to mention the unique and extremely worthwhile crossing of Guajara from the Parador Nacional to Paisaje Lunar (→Alternative), one of the most spectacular hikes on the island!

From the **Parador Nacional**, follow the main road in the direction of Vilaflor and after 200 m turn left at the sign »*Los Roques*« onto a street that ends at a barrier at a little stone hut of the national park administration (15 min, limited parking; you can also walk directly here via a trail from the Parador).

A track continues to the left, circumventing the **Piedras Amarillas** (»Yellow Rocks«) – occasionally, you can see climbers clinging to the bizarre rock walls

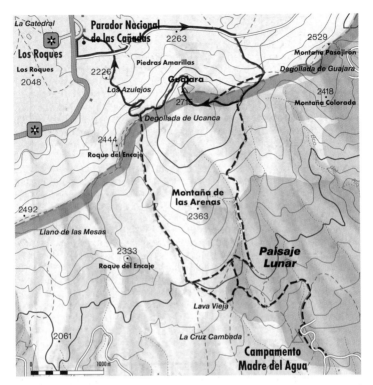

of this craggy metropolis. Later, pass another, less spectacular, formation of crags. In the following left bend, a short-cut path branches off to the right which soon rejoins the track. We are now at the foot of the mighty Guajara. Almost half an hour from the national park hut, ignore a trail branching off to the left which leads to the Teide cable car, then reach the edge of an extensive plain. 5 min later, almost 100 m after the last rocky foothills of Guajara, our ascent path to the Guajara Pass branches off to the right (cairn). Now cairns mark the route which makes a zigzag ascent through the broom shrubs (always remain on the main trail). After almost half an hour, the path forks; continue straight on. 5 min later, reach **Degollada de Guajara**, 2372 m.

To the right, on the ridgeline, an ascending path continues which we ignore (it is a bit shorter but has more scree underfoot). Now walk straight ahead over the crest of the pass and on the other side, bear right along the distinct path leading slightly downhill and soon pass beneath a pretty pumice wall. After a short ascent and a good 5 min later, the ascent route to the summit of Guajara branches off to the right at an iron rod sticking out of the ground (straight on, a possible descent to Paisaje Lunar, →Alternative). The trail is always distinct. Usually bearing to the left, ascend along the slope. After almost half an hour, the trail crosses a precipitous gully and ascends in a straight line. A quarter hour later, reach the highest point on the broad summit plateau of **Guajara** – stone walls offer resting places protected from the wind.

For the descent route, follow the path that descends toward Teide (to the north) – the path starts directly to the right of the large stone wall at the highest point and consistently leads somewhat to the right on the edge of a steep drop-off, sometimes over boulders, down to a small, detached rocky peak with a stone surveyor's marker (a good 5 min). Here, bear sharply to the left to the foot of the summit's northern face. After a short stretch of scrambling, the path leads directly towards the foot of the cliff (almost 10 min) along which it descends steeply, sometimes precipitously but not fully exposed, to the west (some spots require light scrambling over boulders). During the descent over the wide scree and rock outcrop, enjoy a splendid view of the Ucanca plain with Roques de García. After 10 min, the rock outcrop narrows – here at the foot of the cliff, literally bushels of Canarian edelweiss are in bloom. The path now crosses over to a mountain ridge extending down the valley (at the end, the path crosses a scree-filled gully) and then descends along the ridgeline. 45 min from the summit, reach a small group of pines – the path leads to the left through the pines and further along the mountain ridge, down to the nearby **Degollada de Ucanca**, 2408 m (almost 10 min).

View of Guajara from the south.

From the crest of the pass, ascend about 100 m to the west until a distinct path forks off to the right (cairn). This leads for a short distance westward then bends to the right (east) leading directly along the foot of a small, extended rock cliff. Over the next mountain ridge heading toward the valley, descend in tight zigzags onto a light-coloured pumice saddle (½ hr); from here descend to the right to reach the road near the **Piedras Amarillas**. On this road (or on the trail across from it; after 5 min, turn left onto a broad trail, 5 min later turn right onto the path), finally return to the **Parador Nacional**.

48 Paisaje Lunar

To the enchanting minarets and towers of the »lunar landscape«

(Vilaflor –) Campamento Madre del Agua – Paisaje Lunar and back

Location: Vilaflor, 1466 m (bus stop for lines 342/474/482).
Starting point: From Vilaflor, on the main road almost 3 km towards Cañadas, to the right-hand turn-off of the dirt road to Campamento Madre del Agua (next to km 66.0). The pothole-ridden road leads past two dilapidated houses, one after 2.5 km and one after 4.5 km; after 4.9 km, this branches (continue straight on along the major dirt road, sign »Barranco del Río«). After 6.5 km, reach the starting point (1680 m) – here, a walking trail branches off to the left to Paisaje Lunar (sign, parking; from the main road, 1½ hrs on foot, by car about ½ hr).
Walking times: Dirt road – Campamento ½ hr, Campamento – Paisaje Lunar ¾ hr, return route ¾ hr; total time 2 hrs.

Ascent: Almost 300 m.
Grade: Easy walk.
Refreshment: Bar/restaurants in Vilaflor.
Alternative: Excursion to the black lunar landscape (½ hr): At the turn-off of the blue-marked descending trail, straight on uphill and just afterward (at the fork) left on the path passing through a few pines. This ascends traversing the slope (at forks, always remain on the ascending trail lined by stones) and after 15 min, reaches an intersecting trail. Take a right here and continue uphill. The route traverses a slope and crosses over to the Barranco de las Arenas with the black lunar landscape. Here, after 50 m, a marked walking trail branches off to the right to the Guajara Pass ascending the following sand ridge, bearing left.

The lunar landscape is one of the greatest natural wonders on the island: the curious, light-beige coloured towers of pumice stone, resembling minarets, protrude from the slopes on both sides of Barranco de las Arenas, contrasting beautifully with the bright green pine trees – truly a fairyland!

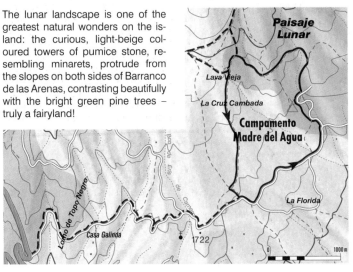

A walker's »dream come true« – the lunar landscape at the southern foot of Guajara.

From the starting point (km 6.5 on the dirt road) follow the dirt road for another 1.7 km (25 min) and then turn left onto a signposted track to reach the **Campamento Madre del Agua**, 1650 m, located 300 m up the road. The track passes to the right of the wooden houses of the holiday camp. After 10 min, we are above the camp – directly after the sharp right-hand bend, a marked path branches off to the left, along which we immediately traverse the small valley to the left and ascend the mountain ridge. After 10 min, reach a height and follow a water conduit to the left. The path traverses a small hill in a *barranco* with several sand ridges sloping down into it. Here, a number of trail spurs branch off to the right but we continue straight on along the water conduit until, about 5 min later, before the last sand ridge and a *galería*, at a boulder (arrow) a distinct path branches off to the right. This leads through a rocky gully and continues always straight on to the nearby **Paisaje Lunar**. The bizarrely formed groups of crags jut up from both sides of the valley.

From the lowest point, a green-marked path ascends to the left. At the upper edge of the group of crags the path turns left, crosses a small valley cleft and then immediately forks. Here, turn left onto the distinct, blue-marked path (straight on, a possible excursion to the black lunar landscape, →Alternative). This leads in a usually gentle descent through the sparse pine wood and you can hardly miss it. After about 40 min, reach a major trail junction (sign »Paisaje Lunar«). Here, turn left onto the broad walking trail lined with stones and head back down to the dirt road (5 min).

49 Sombrero de Chasna, 2411 m

Short, panoramic route on the rocky »hat« (*sombrero*) above Vilaflor

Vilaflor–Cañadas road, km 59.7 – Sombrero de Chasna – Barranco de la Magdalena – Vilaflor–Cañadas road

Location: Vilaflor, 1466 m (bus stop for lines 342/474/482).

Starting point: Two dilapidated stone houses, 2050 m, at a left-hand bend and to the right of the main road Vilaflor–Cañadas, at km 59.7 (8.5 km from Vilaflor and 1.2 km below the Las Lajas picnic area).

Walking times: Main road – caldera rim 1 hr, caldera rim – Sombrero ¼ hr, return route 1 hr; total time 2¼ hrs.

Ascent: A good 400 m.

Grade: Via a distinct path in a sometimes somewhat confusing terrain. At the summit, a short stretch of scrambling (I).

Refreshment: Bar/restaurants in Vilaflor.

Alternative: From the saddle at the caldera rim (between two cairns) a possible descent to the Cañadas road (40 min).

The Sombrero de Chasna is one of the most striking peaks of the caldera rim. Shaped like a hat, the steep rock cliff rises up from the flank of the caldera, blanketed by a sparse pine wood. As to be expected, along the vast summit plateau, the route is rich in panoramic views; at the end, a bit of scrambling is required.

About 20 m below the left-hand bend in the road and passing the lower stone house, a distinct path marked with white arrows and cairns begins the ascent (»TS 10« is painted on the house). Bearing right and traversing the slope almost on the level, the path then continues ascending in zigzags and forks after not quite 5 min – here continue a steep ascent to the left and repeat this manoeuvre at the next fork (watch for the white arrows). A few minutes later, reach the top of a mountain ridge – continue the climb along this. Soon, the path ascends pleasantly in zigzags; the open pine wood provides an almost unlimited view of the southern coast. After walking half an hour, the Sombrero de Chasna appears before us. The white-marked path continues along the mountain ridge – with a view of Barranco de la Magdalena to the right which lies between us and the summit. Soon, pass to the right of a pine tree with broadly spreading branches and surrounded by a stone wall then head directly for a dramatic, dark lava cliff face, passing below this to the right in a short traverse of the slope. The path crosses a scree gully and then ascends on the steep, sandy and scree-covered gully to the nearby ridgeline of the caldera rim. From there, relish a sweeping panorama of the Cañadas.

Sombrero de Chasna – when seen from Vilaflor, it earns its epithet.

Now follow the distinct path near the caldera rim for almost 5 min to the right onto a small saddle. Here, leave the white-marked Caldera Rim Trail behind by bearing right along an indistinct cairn-marked path which leads diagonally to the left onto the saddle at the foot of the first crags of **Sombrero de Chasna**. Circumvent this first group of rocks to the left and then ascend along a white-marked path through a rocky gully, keeping left, to the summit plateau (a bit of scrambling; make a mental note of the entry onto the plateau for the return route!). You should not fail to walk along to the southern edge of the summit plateau – the view of the southern coast and Vilaflor is magnificent; the islands of Gran Canaria, El Hierro and La Gomera are also visible in the distance.

After a good long rest, return to the saddle in front of the first group of rocks (a good 5 min). Here, bear left at the fork and continue to the left on the white-marked path (cairns) descending into a valley that indicates the beginning of **Barranco de la Magdalena**. After 5 min, pass below an eye-catching, bizarrely-formed boulder that looks almost like a miniature version of the »Finger of God«. Almost 5 min later, the path changes to the left flank of the valley, only to return a few minutes later to the right flank. Here the path turns right, in a long traverse, but gradually descends again, not quite down to the floor of the *barranco*. Now the path leaves the valley once and for all; traversing the slope, keep bearing right (usually a gentle descent) crossing over to a mountain ridge (always bear right at forks when in doubt). After another 5-min traverse, reach the approach trail and return along this in a few minutes to the starting point.

50 Huevos del Teide and Montaña Blanca, 2750 m

To the mighty volcanic spheroids at the foot of Teide

El Portillo – Roque del Peral – Huevos del Teide – Montaña Blanca – Huevos del Teide (– Cañada de los Guancheros) – El Portillo

Starting point: Centro de Visitantes (National Park Visitor Centre) in El Portillo, 2050 m, 250 m after the road intersection at the bar/restaurant »El Portillo« (bus stop for lines 342/348).

Walking times: El Portillo – Roque del Peral 20 min, Roque del Peral – Teide track a good 1½ hrs, Teide track – Montaña Blanca ¾ hr, return route 2 hrs; total time 4¾ hrs.

Ascent: A good 700 m.

Grade: Uncomplicated but strenuous walk.

Alternative: Possible descent on the Teide track to the Cañadas road, km 40 (a good 1 hr from Montaña Blanca; bus stop for lines 342/348).

Return via Cañada de los Guancheros: On the ascent trail, retrace for a good ½ hr until a path forks to the left (not quite 5 min from the Teide track). The path heads straight toward Fortaleza and 150 m on passes directly to the left of two »Teide eggs«. Some minutes later, the path bears left passing between a couple of boulders and then immediately drops to the right into a valley and descends in a good hour to Cañada de los Guancheros (always remain to the left of the valley floor and watch for cairns). In the alluvial plain at the foot of Fortaleza, bear right to reach the broad trail that returns in just under 1 hr to El Portillo via Roque del Peral (→Walk 12).

Combination possible with Walks 43 and 51.

The mysterious creation of the »Eggs of Teide«, giant spheroids of lava with a diameter of up to five metres, has not yet been satisfactory determined. Most likely, these separated from a flowing lava mass and when rolling downhill, formed into spherical shapes. The gleaming black *huevos* lay scattered around the light-coloured pumice slope as if strewn by a Goliath's hand.

An unique contrast – the jet-black Huevos and the beige pumice.

The trail begins directly to the left of the **Centro de Visitantes**, passes beneath a small overlook, leads through a gate in a fence and then heads straight towards Teide in constant up-and-down walking (always continue straight on). After 20 min, somewhat below **Roque del Peral**, our trail merges into an intersecting trail: turn sharply to the left. 200 m on (3 min) a distinct path (»Sendero 6«) forks to the right next to a stone bench.

The path heads straight towards Teide, ascending gently over the light beige-coloured pumice sand terrain. After half an hour, pass a conspicuous dark hillock of lava sand to the right of the trail – the **Montaña de los Tomillos**. Not quite ¼ hr later, the trail ascends somewhat more steeply through a small valley gap that is soon flanked to the right by crags. At a small saddle (¼ hr) the trail levels out again. Now it leads towards the saddle between Teide and Montaña Blanca by bearing slightly to the right and then begins to climb more steeply through the pumice slopes after a good quarter hour. After a 10-min ascent, a distinct footpath intersects the trail (to the right, a descent possible to Cañada de los Guancheros, →Alternative). Some minutes later, by two metal posts, our trail merges into the Teide track ascending from the left from the Cañadas road (»Sendero 7«).

Climbing the track in wide bends, pass the **Huevos del Teide** – along the trail, you may also find some extremely rare Teide violets as well as blue »tower of jewels« plants. After half an hour on the track, the sign-posted ascent trail to the Teide summit branches off to the right. Our track, however, leads in a left-hand bend to the nearby summit plateau of **Montaña Blanca** (¼ hr). From there, enjoy a sweeping panoramic view of the Cañadas and the Teide approach trail.

51 Pico del Teide, 3718 m

Ascent to the highest mountain in Spain

Cañadas road, km 40 – Huevos del Teide – Montaña Blanca – Refugio de Altavista – Cueva del Hielo – Teide and back

Starting point: Cañadas road at km 40, 2350 m (between El Portillo, 8 km, and Teleférico, 2.5 km), at the turn-off of the track towards Teide (sign).

Walking times: Cañadas road – path fork at Montaña Blanca 1¼ hrs, ascent to Refugio de Altavista 1 h, Refugio de Altavista – summit terminus of the Teide cable car 1 h, summit terminus of the Teide cable car – Teide summit ½ h, descent 3 hrs; total time 7 hrs.

Ascent: 1400 m (a good 900 m to reach Refugio de Altavista).

Grade: Until reaching Montaña Blanca, a pleasant ascent along a track then an often steep scree-slippery trail; the final summit approach should definitely not be undertaken in stormy weather (some stretches are extremely precipitous). In the winter months, expect snow and also often sheets of ice, frozen rock-solid, making the ascent much more difficult and even requiring special equipment like crampons and an ice axe. In inclement weather (fog, snow, ice, storm), we strongly discourage you from attempting the Teide ascent. Do not take altitude sickness lightly: if, during the ascent, you experience headache, nausea and dizziness, take a rest – if the symptoms persist, we recommend that you turn around.

Food and Accommodation: Refugio de Altavista, 3260 m. The hut was established in 1893 and is staffed year-round, closed only during periods of snow and ice in the winter (tel. 922 23 98 11 or 901 501 901 –

50 beds, running water, cooking facilities, wool blankets available; the emergency accommodation in the annex is open year-round). Reservations are absolutely required; if all the beds are taken, you have to sleep on the floor or outdoors (especially crowded from June – November).

Cable car: The Teide cable car (first summit ascent at 9 a.m., last return to the valley at 5 p.m.) is closed during storms and when the peak is covered by snow and/or ice – be sure to inquire before beginning the route if you intend to use the cable car (tel. 922 69 40 38).

Important note: The trail from the cable car summit terminus to the peak (Teleforo Bravo) is closed to protect the natural terrain – therefore, anyone not prepared to forego the last 160 m of ascent and the peak experience, must apply personally in advance for a special permit at the Oficina del Parque Nacional, Calle Emilio Calzadilla 5, 4th floor, in Santa Cruz (remember to bring copies of your passport and those of your companions; open Monday – Friday, 9 a.m. – 2 p.m.). Warm clothing, wind-and-rain wear, gloves and head covering (even in summer) as well as a good sunscreen are essential. Sufficient food and liquids must be packed along since the Refugio de Altavista does not provide these. For an early morning ascent from the hut to the summit, a hand-held or a head torch is required.

Combination possible with Walks 50 and 52.

The brightly gleaming, in winter sometimes snow-covered Pan de Azúcar, combined with the first-hand experience of a still active, sulphur cloud-enveloped volcano, and last but not least, the thrill of being on the highest mountain in the Canary Islands, in fact, the highest in Spain – all this may well comprise the fascination of this marvellous summit – but one thing certainly takes the prize: the almost unlimited panorama over Tenerife and, in good visibility, over the entire Canary archipelago and as far as Africa. Thus it is no wonder that the ascent of Teide is a dream pursued by many Tenerife holidaymakers.

To get the absolute most out of the summit experience, walkers bent on conquering the peak would do well to divide the four-hour Teide ascent into a two-day trek: on the afternoon of the first day, tackle the most strenuous part of the hike to the Altavista hut. On the following day, begin before daybreak so as to arrive at the summit before sunrise – an unforgettable natural spectacle: within a few minutes, degree by degree, the rising sun bathes the entire island in a deep-red light – at first, Teide, then the caldera rim mountain chain and finally the Cañadas and the Anaga chain – now Teide's shadow is cast all the

way to the neighbouring island of La Gomera, 50 km away! Sensational!

On the **Cañadas road**, at km 40 (parking possible, do not leave valuables in your car!) the signposted track leading to Teide begins (after 100 m – a barrier). The track ascends pleasantly through slopes of light beige-coloured pumice sand. After 15 min, ignore another track forking off to the right (to the left, a possible short-cut along a footpath).

The Refugio de Altavista.

25 min later, by two metal posts, a trail merges sharply from the right, coming from El Portillo (→Walk 50; 100 m further on, a tiny, simple shelter appears to the right below the road). The track now ascends in wide bends through the bright pumice slopes of Montaña Blanca and after a few bends, passes the **Huevos del Teide** (»Eggs of Teide«). After a total of 1¼ hrs, at an elevation of about 2700 m and not far from the summit of **Montaña Blanca**, the signposted path to Refugio de Altavista branches off to the right.

The path ascends in steep zigzags over an ochre-coloured, scree-covered slope; to the left, a dark lava flow slopes downhill. After about half an hour, leaving the steepest part behind, reach a small level area on the slope with gigantic, round boulders – the Estancia de los Ingleses (»Sojourn of the Eng-

View down on the Cañadas – in the centre, Roques de García.

On the summit – view of the neighbouring islands of Gomera, Hierro and La Palma.

lish«). The trail now leads through a vast field of broom which we leave to the left after a quarter hour of walking. Now continue in zigzags then ascend somewhat steeper to reach the **Refugio de Altavista**, 3260 m (½ hr), which seems to pop up before us at the last moment.

To the left of the hut, the broad, sometimes stone-paved trail continues to the summit, ascending sometimes steeply and leading through a lava flow. After about 20 min and immediately after a sharp, left-hand bend, a path branches off to the right, through chunks of lava to the nearby **Cueva del Hielo** (1 min) – descend on an iron ladder into the »Cave of Ice« where icicles hang down from the walls and snow can be found almost year-round. The passages of the extensive lava-flow cave are at least 50 m long. Returning back from the cave, continue ascending on the main trail. The Pan de Azúcar (»Sugar Loaf«), the brightly gleaming cap of Pico del Teide, now comes into view. After not quite half an hour, we come to a level stretch in the slope – the Rambleta – and here meet up with an intersecting panoramic trail. To the right, you can reach **Mirador de la Fortaleza** (5 min) which offers a beautiful view of the eastern part of the island and especially of the Orotava Valley. In the other direction, reach the summit terminus of the **Teide cable car**, 3555 m (a good ¼ hr; from there, the trail continues to Mirador de Pico Viejo, another ¼ hr).

50 m before the terminus, a steep path leads to the right up to the summit. This is also partially stone-paved and, in the uppermost stretch, is somewhat exposed. Bearing right at the rim of the light-coloured crater filled with sulphur vapours, end up at the summit of **Pico del Teide** to relish a nearly boundless view of Tenerife and the outlying islands.

52 Pico Viejo, 3134 m

And yet another volcanic crater to top it off!

Teleférico summit terminus – Mirador de Pico Viejo – Pico Viejo – Narices del Teide – Boca Tauce

Starting point: Summit terminus of the Teide cable car, 3555 m (Teleférico valley terminus, 2356 m, at km 42.5 on the Cañadas road; service to the summit begins at 9 a.m., last return trip to the valley at 5 p.m.; plan for a long wait!). No service during storms or when the peak is covered in snow and/or ice – therefore, inquire in advance if the cable car is running (tel. 922 69 40 38).

Destination: Road intersection at Boca Tauce, 2055 m, at km 53 of the Cañadas road (bus stop for line 342). From there (along the Cañadas road), 7 km to the Parador Nacional, another 3.5 km to Teleférico and another 2.5 km to the turn-off for the Teide ascent route.

Walking times: Cable car summit terminus – Mirador de Pico Viejo at the end of the Rambleta path 15 min, further to Pico Viejo 1¾ hrs, descent to Narices del Teide ½ hr, Narices del Teide – Boca Tauce 1¾ hrs; total time 4¼ hrs.

Descent: From the summit terminus of the Teide cable car a good 1500 m with only short stretches of ascent.

Grade: Difficult, strenuous hike on an indistinct path over lava and scree fields. The path requires absolute sure-footedness and experience in crossing confusing terrain – especially during periods of poor visibility, a good sense of direction is

essential. During the winter months, expect snow and/or ice, which make the descent considerably more difficult. During unfavourable weather conditions (fog, snow, storm), we strongly recommend postponing this mountain hike.

Food and Accommodation: Along the route, no opportunity for food or accommodation – in combination with the Teide ascent (2-day tour), accommodation possible in the Refugio de Altavista, 3260 m (→Walk 51).

Important note: Warm clothing, wind-and-rain protection, gloves and a cap (even in summer) as well as a good sunscreen are recommended. Bring sufficient provisions and enough to drink, especially when staying overnight in the Refugio de Altavista.

Tip: If you arrive with a rental car, it is best to park at Boca Tauce or the Parador Nacional (good overnight accommodations available here) and take bus 342 to Teleférico or to the turn-off of the Teide ascent route (when combined with Walk 51).

Alternative: From Pico Viejo, a possible descent via Roques de García to the Parador Nacional (the trailhead is located at the south-eastern edge of Pico Viejo, between the field of broom and the field of lava sloping down from Teide; scattered cairns, 3 hrs).

Combination possible with Walk 51.

Without exaggeration, the Pico Viejo, the western secondary peak of Teide and, at 3134 m, the second highest summit on the island, can be called one of Tenerife's greatest. With a diameter of 800 m, the mighty crater is not only by far the largest on the island – but also offers a volcanic symphony of colour unique to Tenerife: in it's depths, the palette spans from the deepest black to red and ochre and even to turquoise. The descent route described here, which is sometimes very difficult and mostly leads through volcanic terrain, also subsequently touches on the Narices del Teide (»Teide Nostrils«), massive secondary volcanoes on the southern slope of Pico Viejo. Due to the extreme distance between the starting and finishing points of the walk, but especially due to the enhancement of the experience, we strongly recommend combining this walk with the Teide ascent (Walk 51), staying overnight at the Refugio de Altavista.

From the **summit terminus** of the Teide cable car, follow the left branch of the stone-paved Rambleta path and after 15 min reach **Mirador de Pico Viejo**. Here, the hiking path ends, and to the left, descending through lava flows, a path begins that is at first distinct (cairns). This leads along the wall of a lava

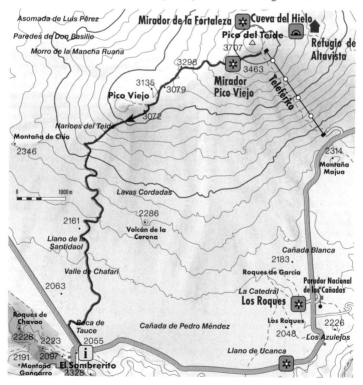

flow and then, after a few minutes, bears left down into a lava valley. Here, pay attention: follow the indistinct path straight on (leading slightly to the right) which descends on and along a wall of the lava flow. After about 25 min, turn to the right and head directly towards the bright pumice slopes of Pico Viejo, now steadily passing through small gullies and over lava ridges, bearing slightly to the right, towards Pico Viejo. We can clearly see the path which leads through the pumice slope marking the saddle between Pico Viejo and Teide, keeping to the left, to Pico Viejo. After a total of 1¼ hrs, finally reach the pumice slope and descend easily along this onto the saddle. On the other side, ascend, keeping left, sometimes between crags, crossing the slope along the rim of the crater and further on to an extensive mountain plateau on the southern rim of the mighty crater. After 45 min, reach the highest point of the plateau, the southern summit, 3107 m, of **Pico Viejo** (large cairn).

Before continuing the descent to Narices del Teide, walk to the western end of the plateau. Here, a magnificent panorama awaits us: below, we can peer into the depths of the dramatic Pico Viejo crater, at this point dropping 200 metres; one can easily descend into the crater from the eastern or the northern side. On the opposite side, enjoy a downwards view of the colourful Narices del Teide. Almost the entire western island now lies at our feet – to the west, the Teno Mountains, as well as vast stretches of the south-west coast and the Cañadas, veined with vividly impressive lava flows, all the way to the Roques de García. A marvellous overlook!

The mighty Pico Viejo crater.

Near the saddle at Pico Viejo – view back to Pico del Teide.

Returning to the cairn at the summit, continue another 30 m and then turn right onto a path marked by cairns and green slashes which bears slightly to the right descending along a slope of volcanic scree. Soon reach the left-hand (southern) edge of an extensive field of broom; a short, rocky stretch follows. Now continue a descent over volcanic scree and sand to the highest and largest crater of the **Narices del Teide** – with a diameter of about 100 m.

30 m on, a distinct path forks away to the left from the left-hand rim of the crater. At first, traverse the slope bearing left then descend more steeply through the scree-covered slope. After 10 min, cross over an intersecting trail coming from Narices. The path continues descending in a fairly straight line. After 10 min and to the right in a neighbouring valley gap, massive volcanic »bombs« can be seen. A good half hour after leaving the Narices crater, the trail merges into a track (about 2300 m) that has already been in view during the descent.

Now continue an easy descent along this track to reach Boca Tauce. Bear right at a fork after 15 min, then not quite 10 min later you can use a path to short-cut a broad bend in the track. 20 min later, another track merges sharply from the left – then after a total of 1¼ hrs, the track merges with the Cañadas road from Chío which, to the left, brings us in 5 min to the road junction at **Boca Tauce**.

Index

157